Virginia Woolf and Anita Desai

Asha Kanwar

Prestige Books
New Delhi

Published by
PRESTIGE BOOKS
3/28, East Patel Nagar, New Delhi 110 008
in association with
Indian Society for Commonwealth Studies
New Delhi

Price:
1989
ISBN 81-85218-07-2

Phototypesetting by
data culture
C-15, Amar Colony, Lajpat Nagar IV
New Delhi 110 065

Printed by
Nirman Press
Delhi 110 006

Contents

INTRODUCTION

And under the oppression of the silent fog
The tolling bell
Measures time not our time, rung by the unhurried
Ground swell, a time
Older than the time of chronometers. . . .

T.S. Eliot

I

Time has a powerful bearing on man's life, emotions, thoughts and experiences. It makes its presence felt on both the physical and the psychic planes of human experience. As in Life, so in Literature, Time asserts itself in one way or the other. The narrative form, be it the epic, the romance or the novel, has always concerned itself with man in action, i.e. man moving in Time. As such, in any form of narrative, Time plays a crucial role, at least, in the structuring of events.

At the turn of the century, we find an almost simultaneous change in the concept of time as enunciated by philosophers and in its treatment by the major novelists of the period like Proust, Woolf, Joyce, and Dorothy Richardson. But it is not a simple case of developments in philosophy influencing those in literature. One can rather look at the whole thing in terms of Goldmann's "homologous relationship" between the current ideas and their expression in literature. Therefore a brief glance at the philosophic theories of time would not be amiss.

The major name here is that of Bergson. Bergson makes a distinction between "clock" time and "psychological" time. Clock time neither "flows" nor "acts" but exists passively like a line drawn on a surface. It represents, in the interests of conformity, arbitrary measurements of duration in terms of standard units like seconds, hours, days etc. Thus it happens to be something objective in essence in contrast to "psychological" time which is essentially subjective. Real Experience, Bergson feels, does not correspond to the mathematical precision of clock-time. We can grasp it only in terms of

> a flowing irreversible succession of states that . . . melt into each other to form an indivisible process. This process is not homogeneous but heterogeneous. It is not abstract but concrete. In short, it is "pure time" or "real duration" (*durée réelle*).[1]

Time and memory are inter-linked concepts. Augustine thinks that the past can be defined only in terms of memories. Bergson makes a distinction between memory and pure memory. Memory, to him, consists of habits that are fixed in the body of the organism and is designed to adapt it to the situation it finds itself in. It is common to both men and animals unlike "pure memory" which is a specific human characteristic. Bergson contends that it retains the whole of our past. That we can be reminded of only a few things at a time is due to the fact that the brain acts as 'a filter for our memories allowing only those that are *practically useful*, to emerge on a given occasion.' [2]

Marcel Proust, on the other hand, looks at memory as either voluntary or involuntary. Voluntary memory produces only conventional and insignificant images whereas involuntary memory transposes man to a plane of being quite independent of his physical existence. It can be triggered off by even trivial sense experiences. It makes available to the human mind the only kind of immortality possible i.e. to grasp (in memory) for a moment what it can never normally get hold of—a bit of time in its pure state (*un peu de temps a l'état pur*).[3] It is a state of immortality, not because it lasts for ever but because it frees us from the fear of death. To Proust, in contrast to Bergson and Freud, the actual memories that return are arbitrary. One memory is as significant as the other. What matters is that one is actually reliving the past at the moment of recalling it. A new plane of being is established as one is *affranchie de l'ordre du temps*. The transforming effect of memory is described by the protagonist in *Swann's Way:*

> I could not be sure first who I was, I had only the most rudimentary sense of existence—I was more destitute of human qualities than the cave dweller; but then . . . memory . . . would come like a rope let down from heaven to draw me up from the abyss of not being . . . in a second I would traverse and surmount centuries of civilisation

and out of a half-visualised succession of oil-lamps, followed by shirts with turned down collars, would put together by degrees the component parts of my ego.[4]

Nicholas Berdyaev's concept of existential time is akin to the Bergsonian durée. Berdyaev makes use of three basic categories—cosmic, historical and existential—to describe time-history in literature. While *cosmic time* refers to the endless recurrence of things, the circularity of natural and human processes, *historical time* refers to the linear course of nations, civilisations and tribes. *Existential time* presupposes the individual's ability to free himself from both cyclic and historical time. It is an extreme form of individualism or in Berdyaev's term"personalism."

Hans Meyerhoff divides time into the public and the private which is again reminiscent of Bergson's concept. But when he says that "so wide is the gap between these two notions of time that each seems to be quite irrelevant to the other,'[5] we tend to disagree for there is no conflict between the two and neither is one superior to the other, as our study will indicate. On the other hand, public time provides the framework within which private time is rendered significant. To quote Ziolkowski, 'The flux of private duration is meaningful only when placed in dialectical opposition to clock or calendar time.'[6]

II

Whatever way time is labelled, as conceptual or perceptual, as *choronos* or *kairos*, its paramount importance to the novelist and his art is undeniable. In fact, 'the genre in conception and practice is so completely committed to time that it ceases to exist if a work is "blown forever outside the loop of time." '[7] Vance Bourjaily rightly points out that the structure of the novel 'come[s] from how you decide to handle time.'[8]

In literature, time shapes can be classified according to their varying relationships to the structure of the work. Higdon enunciates a theory of four time shapes. He points out that each of these shapes can be present in the novel though one of them is often predominant. He talks of *process time* as something distinct from a simple chronological order. It implies that time, as it unfolds, leads to certain developments in a causal sequence, culminating in a particular result. What is stressed here is that events unfold in a causal order and one thing leads to another as in Hardy's *Tess of the D'Urbervilles. Retrospective time* can be summed up in Kierkegaard's maxim 'Life can only be lived forward and understood backward.'[9] Here the character momentarily steps out of the flux of time, considers his past and often changes his complete life-style. Higdon's concept of *barrier time* can best be exemplified through sub-literary forms like fairy tales and T.V. scripts which prescribe a time limit within which a certain task has to be accomplished. The movement is not continuous but constitutes a series of jerks and starts. *Polytemporal time* has the clock-hands running berserk. The author deliberately shuffles time in such a way that a reader often loses track of all time references. There is a dialectical relationship between clock time and "psychological" time with no before and after connections. The narrative moves at various levels, for example, the opening lines of *Mrs. Dalloway* reveal Clarissa in the present, with a sudden jump to the Bourton of thirty years ago and then a flight into the future anticipating Peter Walsh's visit. In *Cry, the Peacock*, Maya constantly delves into the past nightmarish encounter with the albino and breathlessly waits for the evil prophecy to fulfil itself. It is the polytemporal time-shape that is predominant in the works of Woolf and Desai, as our study will reveal.

III

In the polytemporal time-scheme, there is a constant shift from past to present to future. The past is defined in terms of human memories and the future in terms of human expectations. There is an underlying strain of longing for the past, of nostalgia, which surfaces as the shaping spirit of the novels of both Woolf and Desai. It informs not only the content of their work, but shapes the structure as well. For it posits two different times—the present and a longed-for past, upon which the whole novel can be built.

The use of nostalgia, with its frequent references to the past, results in discontinuity indulging our "tendency to reverie" as David Daiches would say and so drawing the reader into the very vortex of the narrative. These shifts are not artificial or superimposed but are a result of the novelist's desire to convey the substance of life, of experience. As a passive reader would be unable to grasp its essence, active reader participation is ensured by the structure of the ncvels. The reader is not passively watching 'that straight line from the first hiccup to the last gasp'[10] but has to bring into play all his faculties to be able to participate in the fictive world of the novels.

Nostalgia is also useful in categorising characters into those who are aware of their past and those who are not. Samuel Butler believes that 'memory and forgetfulness are as life and death to one another. To live is to remember and to remember is to live.'[11] While Gautama, in *Cry, the Peacock* and Richard Dalloway in *Mrs. Dalloway* exist within a clock-bound world, Maya and Clarissa, with their frequent forays into the past, transcend the limits imposed by clock time. According to Bergson, the past is not past but continues into the present through the vehicle of memory. But memory does not recover the past as it was. For each person reconstructs his past in a unique way dependent upon his experiences, prejudices and opinions. Thus the way a character experiences time, helps the reader to grasp the very essence of that character. The characters caught between the past and the present are always in a state of flux, motion and growth. In the works of both Woolf and Desai, the present is being continuously invaded and interrupted by the past. It is memory, the wayward seamstress who 'runs her needle in and out, up and down, hither and thither'[12] stitching the disconnected fragments of experience into an aesthetically pleasing whole. The use of nostalgia then not only determines the author's choice of theme and the way he arranges the elements of his narrative but also regulates his use of language which conveys the experience and meaning of life.

IV

The Victorian time-sense is a fairly simple one uncomplicated by metaphysical concerns. The typical novels of the period are a series of adventures structured in strict chronological sequence. While Dickens takes recourse to the "birth to death" order of narrative, realists like Bennett and Galsworthy adhere to precise clinical detail, causing Woolf to dismiss them as "materialists." For Dickens the only importance of time was that it had a certain "shock value," for it was in "time" that the plot was unravelled, the hero restored and so on. To quote Raleigh:

> What is absent in the Victorians is that more profound sense of the past (deeper than any fascination for the past as picturesque or the past as more attractive socially, in the fashion that Thackeray was intrigued by the 18th century)—the obsession of modern man that the past is continually impinging on the present and assuming the proportions of a nightmare.[13]

With the advent of Hardy and James, time starts to be used in more positive ways. The focus shifts from the present-future juxtaposition to the past-present one. The clock stops, while James explores the novel dimension of time created within the mind of the individual. On the other hand, in Hardy, time is often dramatised as "malignant Fate," waiting to destroy humans.

It is, however, the Jamesian use of time that has affected modern novelists. While, undoubtedly, it had a bearing on the technique of the novels, it also helped in changing the concept of "characterology." For example, in Dickens, the characters are sketched with hard definite outlines, while later writers like Joyce, Proust and Woolf sketch blurred shadowy figures in the manner of the Post-Impressionists.

For Woolf, 'Life is not a series of gig lamps symmetrically arranged; life is a luminous halo, a semi-transparent envelope'[14] and as the writers's function is to represent life, a technique other than the traditional one would have to be adopted. The traditional novel, on the whole, concentrates upon

> outer events and acts taking place within a phenomenological universe, full of things and persons; it assumes the existence of a pattern or purpose. Events are so arranged that significance can be readily deduced from the structure.[15]

The early twentieth century novelists, while not denying the importance of the external, concentrate on the internal and upon the nature of reality as perceived by various psyches. Connections of time and space are displaced by 'a more fundamental search for axiological connections.'[16] Values become extra-temporal and clock-time is subjugated to the inner experience of time which becomes extremely elastic. One day of clock-time can be stretched to seem a hundred years while a whole day can seem to have passed in seconds. Thus real or psychological time may pass quickly or slowly, depending on the emotional states of the character such as excitement and boredom. 'It can contract or expand, contracting to attention on a single present fact or state, or expanding to include simultaneous memories from one or more periods of past time.'[17] The Edwardian novel was felt to neglect psychological for physical detail and to run 'in the current of time and space "without diving deep" into the infinite potentiality of any one moment.'[18] The early twentieth century novelists felt a need for a different concept of time that would, paradoxically, release man from the limits of time itself. To quote Louis Gillet, 'whatever is most valuable in modern literature is a meditation on the nature of time, on the mystery of memory and personality.'[19] Lukacs thus accounts for the emergence of the change in the novelist's attitude towards time and memory:

> Now once again the novel can express a kind of unity of meaning and life, but it is a unity thrust into the past, a unity remembered only. For in the present, the world always defeats the hero, frustrates his longing for reconciliation; yet when he remembers his failure, paradoxically he is at one with it. The process of memory has therefore drawn the resistant outside world into subjectivity, there, in the past, reiterating a kind of unity with it . . . time is profoundly ambiguous in nature, a force both life-giving and life-destroying . . . is also the very fabric of life, for reader as well as for the hero the very substance of experience; it is therefore at once duration and flow, and founds the density of the narrative at the same moment at which the latter tells of the tragic passage and ephemerality of all things.[20]

V

To Woolf, the business of the novelist is the exploration of the human personality so as to attain a vision of life's meaning. Her characters live, think and unfold in time and hence her preoccupation with the problems relating to it. 'This preoccupation underlies her concern with the phenomena of memory, change and death and drives her to ask several different questions.'[21]

There is a dichotomy in Woolf between two types of worlds—one, a world of linear time; the other, of psychological time or *durée*, in which 'the chaotic flow of experience derived from our life in linear time is reduced to order and unity, in which we are therefore liberated.'[22] Woolf was troubled by this conflict to which two solutions are possible—either to accept that both worlds are integrally related or to declare that one is unreal and that in the other only can we find a valid absolute.

Woolf's first two novels follow the traditional pattern in retaining a chronological sequence. *The Voyage Out* is literally a forward movement in space and time from London to Lisbon to Saint Marina. But clock-time is dissolved when memory calls up the past thereby obliterating the present, for example, when Mrs. Ambrose and Mrs. Thornbury simultaneously recall the vision of Mrs. Parry's drawing room. In *Night and Day* too, though the novel progresses in a linear movement, we have a good deal of stress on association and memory, for instance, when Katherine is transported to the hills of Italy stimulated by the evocative title "Isabella and the Pot of Basil," Ralph frequently returns to Katherine's house in his day-dreams. Katherine sometimes feels that 'the past had completely displaced the present, which, when one resumed life after a morning amid the dead proved to be of an utterly thin and inferior composition,'[23] a sentiment echoed in Woolf's last work *Between the Acts.*

In *Jacob's Room*, the present is replaced by the characters' reflections. Jacob's life is constructed by the sense-impressions filtering through various psyches. By an adroit shift of tense, past is mingled with the present tense commentary of the narrator. *Mrs. Dalloway* effectively focuses on the events of one day in the lives of Clarissa Dalloway and Septimus. Big Ben tolling implacably in the background reminds one of the reality of passing time. The restricted framework of a single day is given a multi-dimensional significance by the constant shifts of focus to past and future while remaining anchored to the "here and now." Although ten years elapse between Parts I and III of *To the Lighthouse,* the novel follows the movement of a single day. The afternoon and evening of the first part are followed by the dark night of the second section and the early morning of the third. Here the world of psychological time and the world of linear time are related to each other because both are related to a central reality. Apart from this, there is a thread of nostalgia running throughout the novel.

Orlando stretches over a passage of 350 years while the hero/heroine ages only twenty. This is not only wilful flaunting of the limits of time but a pointer to the fact that Woolf felt that 'external, linear chronologies have little to do with the inner experience of time which can be complicated, paradoxical and totally at variance with how things appear on the surface.'[24] The nine poetic interludes of *The Waves* describe the progression of the sun through the passage of a single day. The six speakers carry on their monologues in a rarefied atmosphere that is extra-spatial and extra-temporal. The passage of the day closely parallels the different stages of experience of the speakers. Memory helps them transcend their limits of mortality a la Proust and Percival lives long after he has fallen dead on the dusty plains of India.

In *The Years*, we have explicitly dated chapters moving from 1880 to the present. To quote Guiguet:

> The meeting of the past and present, defining differences as well as similarities, is crucial to the novel, dramatising as it does the central question of what changes and what remains the same, of how we experience the vagaries of our own identities and those of others.[25]

Between the Acts takes place within the confines of twenty-four hours (a favourite limit that Woolf imposes upon herself). But the sense of time is demolished by Miss La Trobe's pageant that covers a space of centuries and while watching it, the characters wander down memory lane to give the reader the knowledge of all that has preceded the action. Thus we can say with Harvena Richter that 'Time for Virginia Woolf was not measured by the clock but experienced emotionally—hence the phrase "moment of being."'[26] Though consciously not a Bergsonian, Woolf subscribes to his concept of *durée,* in which time can expand or contract independent of its mechanical aspect. She can be dubbed Proustian too in that her characters not only remember the past but also live in it, thus creating for themselves a plane of existence independent of quotidian reality.

While *A Writer's Diary* lays open before us Virginia Woolf's mind, there is no such extensive document which could throw light upon the underlying theories of Desai's work. To do so, we shall have to depend upon the few interviews that she has given and also try to deduce her "theories" from her work itself. Desai claims:

> A writer does not create a novel by observing a given set of theories—he follows flashes of individual vision, and depends on a kind of instinct that tells him what to follow and what to avoid; how to veer away from what would be destructive to his vision.[27]

Therefore a brief resumé of the use of time and memory in her novels is essential to help us grasp the "vision" that underlies her creative work.

Woolf, in most of her novels, operates within the framework of clock-time. Even though the characters are allowed to drift freely on their stream of consciousness, the ticking of the clock is never out of hearing. Desai, except in *Where Shall We Go this Summer ?*, has no such temporal framework. *Cry, the Peacock* is divided into three parts which can be literally described as the beginning, the middle and the end. Part II lays bare the protagonist's mind in the manner of Woolf. Maya's journey down the corridor of years is not golden and idyllic for in the shadows lurks the image of the frightful albino jeopardising the chances of future happiness. Maya is a helpless prisoner in the ineluctable clutches of the tyrant, time.

Voices in the City is a series of pieces of a jigsaw puzzle that have to be pieced together in order to get a composite view of the four parts, each dedicated to the four major characters. Though the major concern of the novel is 'the terror of facing, single-handed the ferocious assaults of existence'[28] to quote Ortega y Gasset, yet memory and nostalgia posit the past and present in a dialectical confrontation. Somy's father recounts incidents of his glorious but decadent past and contrasts them with the aridity of the present and the bleakness of the future. Here the preference for an idyllic past smacks strongly of similar sentiments expressed in Woolf's *Night and Day* and *Between the Acts*.

Bye-Bye Blackbird, though predominantly concerned with the existential problem of loneliness and adjustment in an alien land, is drenched in nostalgia. Adit, an Anglophile to begin with, ultimately succumbs to the pangs of nostalgia for his homeland. The far removes of space and time cannot keep him from visiting, at least in memory and imagination, the vast and wild landscapes of India. His nostalgia acquires a dreadful dimension of "an illness, an ache" in him and hounds him back to a search for his roots.

Where Shall We Go This Summer ? is amazingly similar in structure to *To the Lighthouse*. Like it, it is also divided into three parts—

Part I, Monsoon '67, Part II, Winter '47, Part III, Monsoon '67. Part I has Sita living in her present and immediate past while Part II goes back to her remote past and childhood, Part III deals with the question of her future. Sita's second visit to the island is a failure as she tries to cling to the glory of the past ignoring the fact that time is a great destroyer.

Fire on the Mountain is also divided into three parts. The first part has Nanda Kaul living in perfect isolation in her hilltop retreat Carignano. The past clings to her and has made her what she is—a cynic better left alone. Raka the introvert, is haunted by visions of her violent father and whimpering mother. Ila Das has seen better days, the memory of which only heightens the truly pathetic state of her present. While Ila wishes to escape to her happy past, Nanda wishes to turn away from her tragic past into the colourful world of fabricated stories. The two friends have been treated differently by time the destroyer and time the preserver.

Clear Light of Day is a novel divided into four parts. Parts I and IV deal with the present interspersed with past memories while Part II is devoted to the partition scenario. Part III takes us to the childhood of the Das children. Desai illustrates how time can corrode the best of all relationships like the one Bim and Raja shared and how time again can soften the rancour and heal the scars. She thus sums up her concept of time vis-a-vis *Clear Light of Day*, 'Basically my preoccupation was with recording the passage of time.... My novel is about time as a destroyer, as a preserver and about what the bondage of time does to people.'[29] This is equally true of her other novels. The "existential" concern of time in relation to eternity is throughout discernible in her works. We quote a passage from the novel:

> She saw how her own house and its particular history linked and contained her as well as her whole family with their separate histories and experiences ... not binding them ... but giving them the soil in which to send down their roots.... That soil contained all time, past and future, in it. It was dark with time, rich with time.[30]

And as if this does not explain the concept sufficiently, Desai clarifies in an interview with Yashodhara Dalmia:

> I mean the human condition itself. It is only superficially affected by the day-to-day changes. We continue to live in the same way as

> we have in the past centuries with the same tragedies and the same comedies."[31]

The only way to create a sense of meaning in the face of such hopelessness is to relive the past in the Proustian way.

'Since all art presupposes a degree of selection and presentation . . . the perspectives of the writer become the formative principles of his art.'[32] In both Woolf and Desai, we find an almost obsessive involvement with the characters' past as a key to their consciousness, their life. A preoccupation with Nostalgia and Memory thus becomes an integral part of their craft. But these are not used as things in themselves. They are used artistically both for thematic as well as formal purposes. A careful study of the novels will make us understand how they are made to function as artistic tools.

NOTES

1. P. Edwards, ed., *The Encyclopaedia of Philosophy* (London, 1967), p.288.
2. Ibid., My italics.
3. Ibid., p. 289.
4. Marcel Proust, *Swann's Way, Remembrance of Things Past,* Vol. I, quoted in Lisa Ruddick, *The Seen and the Unseen: Virginia Woolf s To The Lighthouse* (Cambridge, 1977), pp. 7-8.
5. Hans Meyerhoff, *Time in Literature,* quoted in Higdon, *Time and English Fiction* (London, 1977), p. 2.
6. Higdon, p. 136.
7. Ibid., p.10.
8. Vance Bourjaily,"A Certain Kind of Work," in *Afterwords*, ed. Thomas McCormack, quoted in Higdon, p. 3.
9. Higdon, p. 6.
10. William Golding, *Free Fall* (New York, 1959), p. 6.
11. Butler quoted in Allen McLaurin, *Virginia Woolf: The Echoes Enslaved* (Cambridge, 1973), p. 4.
12. Virginia Woolf, *Orlando* (London, 1977), p. 49.
13. J.H. Raleigh, "The English Novel and the Three Kinds of

Time," *Perspectives in Contemporary Criticism*, ed. Grebstein (New York, 1968), p. 43.

14. Virginia Woolf, *The Common Reader* (London, 1968), p. 189.

15. M.A. Goldberg, "Chronology, Character and the Human Conditions: A Reappraisal of the Modern Novel," *Criticism*, Vol. V, No.1, Winter 1963, p. 3.

16. Ibid.

17. Harvena Richter, *Virginia Woolf: The Inward Voyage* (New Jersey, 1978), p. 39.

18. Ruddick, p. 23.

19. Louis Gillet, quoted in Jean Guiguet, *Virginia Woolf and Her Works*, tr. Jean Stewart (London, 1965), p. 382.

20. Frederick Jameson, *Marxism and Form* (New Jersey, 1971), pp. 176-177.

21. John Graham, "Time in the Novels of Virginia Woolf," *Critics on Virginia Woolf*, ed. Jacqueline E.M. Latham (Florida, 1970), p. 28.

22. Ibid.

23. Virginia Woolf, *Night and Day* (London, 1978), p. 38.

24. Michael Rosenthal, *Virginia Woolf* (London, 1979), p. 139.

25. Guiguet, p. 182.

26. Richter, p. 38.

27. Atma Ram, "An Interview with Anita Desai," *World Literature Written in English*, Vol. 16, No.1, April 1977. p. 100.

28. Madhusudan Prasad, *Anita Desai: The Novelist* (Allahabad, 1981), p. 57.

29. Interview by Sunil Seth, *India Today*, Dec. 1-15, 1980, p. 142.

30. Anita Desai, *Clear Light of Day* (Harmondsworth, 1980), p. 182.

31. *The Times of India*, April 29, 1979, p. 13.

32. V. Kannabiran, *The Marxist Theory of Fiction* Unpublished M. Litt. dissertation (CIEFL, Hyderabad), p. 10.

MRS. DALLOWAY and *CRY, THE PEACOCK*

I cannot but remember such things were
That were most precious to me.

Macbeth

Virginia Woolf and Anita Desai are rooted in two totally different milieus. Yet the works of the two share not only in structure (*Where Shall We Go This Summer ?* and *To the Lighthouse*) and themes (loneliness, isolation, death etc.) but also in imagery (reality being like an iceberg, snails, the fin etc.). It is not the simple case of the younger writer, Desai in this case, aping an illustrious predecessor but a testimonial to the time-transcending nature of artistic sensibility.

Mrs. Dalloway, the fourth novel by Virginia Woolf, follows the trend of complete break from conventional techniques that started with *Jacob's Room.* It carries all the traits characteristic of Woolf's novels—stream of consciousness, internal monologue, a poetic style, suppression of plot, suppression of objective character descriptions and camera-eye technique. Anita Desai, too, has the unusual distinction of making it to the Hall of Fame with her first novel *Cry, the Peacock.* Seen in a wider context, it is a sensitive study of Man's predicament in a hostile universe. It is remarkable for its poetic style, its internal monologues and above all for its vivid and colourful creation of the Indian landscape, not for its own sake but as an "objective correlative" to the state of mind of the characters.

The novels of both Woolf and Desai reveal their pre-occupation with Time. It informs both the thematic and the formal aspects of their novels. In *Mrs. Dalloway* and *Cry, the Peacock,* we encounter, to use Higdon's phrase, the polytemporal time shape. It is closely allied, in principle, to the modern art of Cezanne, Picasso and Dali. In it, temporal boundaries, that had constituted the basic principle of narrative art since Aristotle, hardly exist. The narrative moves up and down through layers of time. As Durrell puts it:

> The narrative momentum forward is counter-sprung by references backwards in time, giving the impression of a book which is not travelling from '*a*' to '*b*' but standing above time and turning slowly on its own axis to comprehend the whole pattern . . . a marriage of past and present with the flying multiplicity of the future racing towards one.[1]

Though the main time-scheme of the two novels is polytemporal, in *Cry, the Peacock*, we can discern the "barrier" time-shape as well. The albino predicts 'death—an early one—by unnatural causes' (*CTP*, p. 30) four years after Maya's marriage and as time passes, the gruesome prediction comes to fulfil itself within the prescribed time limit.

It is difficult to imagine a Dickens or a Hardy writing a novel covering a time-span of one day only. Such writers need several years to develop their characters and to conclude their narratives. For Woolf, however, the confines of a single day offer the best scope for her genius as is evident from the fact that her best works cover, literally or metaphorically, only one day. *Mrs. Dalloway* opens on a "day in June" and ends the same evening when at Clarissa's party, the parallel strands of the Clarissa and Septimus stories are linked together in an aesthetically pleasing unity. In *Cry, the Peacock*, we have the spring to summer framework. The novel opens in a haze of April heat and ends soon after the summer "loo" stormily sweeps away Maya's last tenuous link with sanity.

In *Mrs. Dalloway*, the narrative flows smoothly without the hindrance of demarcation into chapters. *Cry, the Peacock*, on the other hand, is divided into three parts. The first part can be viewed as the prologue which more or less anticipates the epilogue, both sections being balanced by death. These two parts are entirely taken over by the omniscient narrator while the second part is given to Maya. In *Mrs. Dalloway* the omniscient narrator obtrudes off and on while the main narrative flows on through the minds of the various characters.

Frank Swinnerton's remark that 'Hating story, denying story, Mrs. Woolf tries to do without story' is equally applicable to Desai. Neither of them employs a story with a beginning, a middle and an end. In fact, their technique is somewhat similar to Oskar's meditations on how to begin his story in Gunter Grass's *The Tin Drum.* He decides "you can begin a story in the middle and create confusion by striking out boldly, backward and forward."[2] They deal not with the sensational and the momentous but with the ordinary experiences of life. What they present are moments in the lives of their characters, chained to each other by memories. Thus it is through a skilful use of time and memory that the themes of the two writers are developed and given a pattern.

By showing the arid present in contrast with the idyllic past, Woolf and Desai stress the theme of an individual's isolation. In their works, the present is saturated with and inseparable from the past. Just as in human experience, one must lose a thing to realise its full value, so in art, the lost past is viewed with a sense of longing. Nostalgia leads to discontent with one's present. Clarissa in *Mrs. Dalloway*, regrets her passionless marriage to Richard and longs for the happiness that might have been hers, had she married Peter. Similarly, in *Cry, the Peacock* Maya's fruitless marriage to Gautama with its lack of emotional attachment stands in sharp contrast to her affection-filled childhood.

Clarissa, to start with, exults in the present but with Peter on the scene, an uneasy dissatisfaction sets in. She starts looking with nostalgia at her past and experiences a feeling of isolation. Similarly Maya, who revels in the colours, sounds and sensations of the here and now, cannot wipe off the shadow of the past. From her window, Clarissa sees people passing 'each moving under the compulsion of the time-flow (as symbolised by Big Ben) visible to each other, yet unknown to each other and essentially alone.'[3] This lack of understanding and communication between individuals is echoed in Maya's words, 'There was not one of my friends who could act as an anchor any more, and to whomsoever I turned for resources, betrayed me now.' (*CTP*, p. 64) Neither father, nor husband, nor friends can remove this terrible feeling of desolation.

Past hopes and present achievements are sadly "out of joint" for the various characters. In *Mrs. Dalloway*, Peter, who had hoped for a poetic career confesses to Sally Seton at Clarissa's party that so far, he had written "not a word." Clarissa's hopes of becoming the prime minister's wife are lost forever as her mediocre politician husband misses a place in the Cabinet. Maya, in *Cry, the Peacock*, had felt that marriage would be a continuation of her rosy childhood with Gautama playing the indulgent father-role. But time implies flux and to quote Southwell:

Times go by turns, and chances change by course
From foul to fair, from better hap to worse.[4]

The passage of time also signals the final end of man. Thus death becomes another of the common themes of the two writers. In *Mrs. Dalloway*, the tolling of the Big Ben reminds the characters of the inexorable passage of time. Clarissa repeats to herself ' if it were now to die, 'twere now to be most happy.' (p. 39 and pp. 203-204) While the characters are often allowed to transcend time by taking recourse to memory, the repeated intrusion of public time does not let them forget their mortality. Big Ben tolls the death knell for Septimus and metaphorically also for Clarissa who, though physically alive, realises that her soul is dead. But this realisation paradoxically, sets her beyond the limits of time. Similarly, death is never far from Maya in *Cry, the Peacock.* Entering the fourth year of her marriage, she cannot rid herself of the albino nightmare.

Ensconsed in her secluded attic room, Clarissa strips off her societal masks and finds herself a straw adrift the ebb and flow of time. For her, the memories of girlhood are full of carefree jaunts with Sally and Peter. Bourton is a haven and Peter a longed-for memory. Maya's childhood, however, is not totally idyllic. She is nostalgic for the cheerful days when her childhood concerns were centred on her parties, racquet games and a doting father. But the moment she remembers her encounter with the albino, her present is over-shadowed with gloom and foreboding.

The time-dominated individual is set in contrast to the timelessness of the universe. The idea that men may come and men may go but the human race goes on forever is symbolised in the song of the old woman 'ee um fah um so/foo swee too eem oo' (*MD*, p. 90) which is described as 'the voice of no age or sex.' (*MD*, p. 90) This voice seemed to be singing since millions of years and would continue to do so to the very end of civilization. And in *Cry, the Peacock* the 'loo' is described thus:

> Such storms had blown since the time when the earth was desert and no living thing, no creeping, crawling beasts, plants or cells stirred upon that great plain. Such storms would sweep the earth and the last traces of these huge masses of creeping, crawling, toiling, struggling cell-conglomerations that now wracked the earth when the time came for annihilation.

Gautama explains to Maya:

> This life you speak of, this little flash-in-the pan, how insignificant and trivial it appears compared with the immortal cycle to which all humanity is bound. . . . (*CTP*, p. 127)

Desai seems to be referring to 'the endless recurrence of things, night following day, season following season, the cycle of birth, growth and decay; in short the circular character of human and natural experience'[5] for which Nicholas Berdyaev's words would be "cosmic time."

Like Lily Briscoe's painting, the structure of *Mrs. Dalloway* is in perfect harmony. The main events are the passing of the Personage and the advent of the airplane in the beginning, ending with Septmus' suicide and Clarissa's party. Like a line passing down the middle, we have Peter's visit to Clarissa balancing the structure. Joining all these events are the memories evoked by various stimuli. The texture of the single day is enriched by the exquisitely controlled transitions to the past and future and a fusion of the past and present. 'The design is so queer and so masterful,' Woolf writes in her diary, 'I'm always having to wrench my substance to fit it. The design is certainly original and interests me hugely.' [6] Rosenthal commenting on the design writes:

> The primary impact of the design is ironic for the web of interactions occurring both physically in the streets of London— and mentally—in memories and associations of the characters— provides the formal unity of a novel depicting a world in which characters are irrevocably cut off from themselves as well as from one another.[7]

It can be seen that the structural connections stress the sense of disconnectedness experienced by most of the characters. For example, the formal unity and neat transitions from one consciousness to the other heighten the feeling of disharmony and isolation. In *Cry, the Peacock*, the beginning and the end are conventional enough but in Part II we are let adrift Maya's stream of consciousness. The linear sequence of the narrative is frequently broken by Maya's reminiscences in what Conrad Aiken in a different context calls "the deliberately withheld meaning technique" as when Maya needs Arjuna's letter:

> 'Dear Maya . . . Dear Sister, dear small stupid silly sweet sister, it

> said . . . I heard you are married. Impossible to believe, yet it was, of course, the inevitable for you, and I am sure you are very . . .' Strange Arjuna, strange brother . . . I heard this voice again low swift, urgent, when he was serious. . . . (*CTP*, p. 136)

The main skeletal events of Toto's death, the visit to the Lals, the visit of Nila and her mother and the deaths of Gautama and Maya are held together by carefully selected details which juxtapose the past to the present as we are swept towards the inevitable future. As in *Mrs. Dalloway*, the well-balanced structure only serves to accentuate the disarray of Maya's sensitive mind and its irrevocable fall into insanity.

Woolf and Desai generally avoid the conventional devices for character delineation—an objective description of the physical and mental attributes of the characters. They use memory, in a series of internal monologues, to give us access to the characters' minds. Woolf 'sought to represent the essence of character, and the quality of experience without indulging in superficialities.'[8] Clarissa, some people may feel, is described in a somewhat conventional way when Scrope Purvis talks of her as having 'a touch of the bird about her, of the jay, blue-green, light, vivacious, though she was over fifty and grown very white since her illness.' (*MD*, p. 6) But this is not an objective description. It is the impression that Clarissa creates in the mind of Purvis. Woolf explaining her process of characterisation talks of:

> how I dig out beautiful caves, behind my characters. I think that gives exactly what I want, humanity, humour, depth. The idea is that the caves shall connect and each comes to daylight at the present moment.[9]

She adds, 'It took me a year's groping to discover that I call my tunnelling process by which I tell the past by instalments, as I have need of it.'[10] For example, when Clarissa remembers her girlhood fancy of being a prime minister's wife, we conclude that she is a snobbish socialite, an opinion corroborated by Walsh himself. But when she muses on the death of Septimus, the depth of her nature is revealed. The memory of her intense relationship with Sally establishes her androgynous nature. Septimus, an aspiring poet, is shell-shocked out of his wits and his hallucinations and ravings are a comment on the evil effects of civilisation. Like Pierre in

Sartre's 'The Room,' he denies that anything outside even exists and he opts out of the flow of time when he falls on Mrs. Filmer's railings with a 'thud thud thud in his brain.' (*MD*, p. 203) In fact, he may be said to be Clarissa's alter-ego, one complementing the other as it was Woolf's design to 'adumbrate here a study of insanity and suicide; the world seen by the sane and the insane side by side. . . .'[11] At his death Clarissa ruminates:

> She felt somehow very like him—the young man who had killed himself. She felt glad that he had done it; thrown it away while they went on living. The clock was striking. The leaden circles dissolved in the air. (*MD*, p. 206)

Though the two of them never meet, Clarissa reaches out to him across the time and space that separates them.

Walsh's forays into the past depict him as having an incorrigibly roving eye. When Clarissa sees him:

> . . . she recognises in him the old familiar gestures, intonations, habits of speech and of thought and memories flood back on her; and gradually, by means of these memories, the past is reconstructed for the reader.[12]

In the reminiscences of Lady Bruton and Peter Walsh, Richard Dalloway appears as an earnest though unsuccessful politician. Thus the essence of the characters is revealed in a few light strokes. No neat labels can compartmentalise them for as Mrs. Dalloway, sounding much like Virginia Woolf herself, says, 'She would not say of anyone in the world now that they were this or were that,' (*MD*, p. 50) a sentiment similar to the one expressed by the narrator in *Jacob's Room*, 'Its no use trying to sum people up' (*JR*, p. 28) as all human beings are subject to the flux of time and change.

On the other hand, Desai, by recording the different reactions of Gautama and Maya to Toto's death, objectively establishes, at the very outset, the identities of her two characters. Maya lives intensely for each moment. Gautama, the remote, detached intellectual is bewildered by her hypersensitiveness. He preaches the ideal of the Gita but Maya feels this calm to be the very negation of life. She emerges as the hypersensitive daddy's darling, who never grows up while Gautama is depicted as the unfeeling rationalist. Having established these premises, we are turned over to Maya's consciousness, and her frequent broodings over the past inform us about the previous events in a somewhat Ibsenian manner. Just as Ibsen keeps his dramas within the boundaries of time and space but draws upon his characters' memories so that all that is relevant to their past lives is unfolded for the audience, so Desai, like Woolf, allows the reader a glimpse into the past through the characters memories. Time has been kinder to Clarissa than it has been to Maya. Clarissa, at fifty, has a husband who loves her, an attractive daughter and all the trappings of a comfortable life. Maya, about half her age, is childless and bereft of the love that she so yearns for. Her memories of the bear episode and her reaction to it, establishes her neurosis beyond doubt and as she gradually deteriorates into madness, her memories become wilder and repetitive and her hallucinations remind one of Septimus. Maya is a combination of Clarissa and Septimus. She is like Clarissa in that she loves life and the sensations of the moment while her constant flashbacks of the albino episode and hallucinations of the drums and the Kathakali dancer gone berserk, call to mind similar visions of the dead Evans in Septimus. Thus from the characterisation, it can be easily inferred that both Woolf and Desai believe that a person's past is inseparable from his personality and continually informs his present.

The use of nostalgia also affects the narrative technique and style of the two writers. Let us examine the following passage from *Mrs. Dalloway:*

> Lady Bruton raised the carnations, holding them rather stiffly with much the same attitude with which the general held the scroll in the picture behind her; she remained fixed, tranced, which was she now, the general's great-grand daughter ? great great grand-daughter ? Richard Dalloway asked himself. Sir Roderick Sir Miles Sir Talbot—that was it. It was remarkable how in that family the likeness persisted in the woman.... He knew her country. He knew her people. There was a vine, still bearing, which either Lovelace or Herrick—she never read a word of poetry herself, but so the story ran, had sat under. Better wait to put before them the question that bothered her (about making an appeal to the public), if so, in what terms and so on), better wait until they have had their coffee, Lady

> Bruton thought, and so laid the carnations down beside her plate. (*MD*, pp. 116-117)

The physical scene is first described objectively. Then the focus shifts to Richard's reflection of the same and on to the mind of Lady Bruton and from her speculation on her future course of action, it is rounded off by the shift back to the physical scene. These transitions demand different responses from the reader. The reader is moved smoothly from the external to the internal, from the present to the past and from one mind to another, to experience not just one sensation but to experience 'a shower of atoms' that is hurled on his mind.

A passage from *Cry, the Peacock* with a somewhat similar technique is worth examining at length:

> "No ?" Gautama was surprised. He sat over the tea-tray, rubbing his hands. "You look disappointed." He looked at me, waiting. I did not move. So he shrugged, poured out his tea. Yes, it was best for him to learn how to do it himself. One of us would be left alone to always pour out his or her tea, in loneliness; I felt the shroud of death blur my vision, while through it I saw him sitting, miles away in the distance, squeezing out a small, yellow lemon that filled the stale air with a sharp, shooting odour of astringent freshness. The limes that shaded the dog's corpse had emitted just such an odour upon a fine spring evening, long ago. Death and youth, stillness and sensation. "Who was the letter from then," he asked, settling back comfortably with a cup of tea. He had had a good day in the courts, hence his excellent mood. (*CTP*, p. 142)

Here again the paragraph begins and ends in an objective description. From Gautama's pouring out tea, the reader is led to Maya's vision of future loneliness. The smell of the lemon transports her back to the past and the dead Toto, she cannot forget. In both Woolf and Desai, the psychology of association is nicely demonstrated with the reader being made to participate successfully in the characters' movements back and forth in time.

In a letter to Jacques Raverat, the painter, Woolf described 'how she wished to achieve the splash effect of a painter in her use of language, rather than the strictly linear "railway line" type of sentence of Bennett and Galsworthy.'[13] She needed the right language to go with her concept of time. Hence her use of several asides which serve to underscore time and place.

> How fresh, how calm, stiller than this of course, the air was in the early morning, like the flap of a wave, the kiss of a wave; chill and sharp and yet (for a girl of 18 she was then) solemn, feeling as she did. . . . (*MD*, p. 5)

The feeling is translated into the image of a flapping and kissing wave and it gives her prose a poetic aura. Here the style is dictated by the memory of her past life in Bourton—with all the lyricism and poetry of youth. The very description of time becomes poetic. Observe the alliteration in 'the sound of bells, striking the hour or singing to service, as a single spider thread is blotted with rain-drops, and, burdened, sags down.' (*MD*, p. 124) The phrase 'Fear no more the heat of the sun' from Shakespeare's dirge recurs several times through Clarissa's reverie and it is echoed in Septimus' nightmare, thus linking the worlds of "the sane and the insane,"[14] as Woolf called it in her diary.

The use of nostalgia and memory signals the use of some words more than others, "for" being a favourite with Woolf. Clarissa's musings at her party:

> It was so extraordinarily nice of them to have come ! But talk of dancing ! The rooms were packed. There was old Aunt Helena in her shawl. Alas, she must leave them—Lord Grayton and Nancy Blow. . . .
>
> For Miss Helena Parry was not dead. Miss Parry was alive . . . where had Peter got to. They used to be such friends. (*MD*, p. 197)

Here "for" connects the different stages in the memory of the character, "for", as Daiches explains, being 'a word which does not indicate a strict logical sequence . . . but does suggest a relationship which is at least half-logical.'[15]

In order to communicate the continuity of memory, Woolf makes frequent use of present participles of action. (Such fools, we are, she thought, crossing Victoria street). This Daiches explains is 'to allow the author to remind the reader of the character's position, without interrupting the thought stream.'[16] Lodge criticises these devices as leading to monotonous repetition. The two elements of Woolf's style i.e. the observation of the external world and the description of moods are dictated by her use of public and private time respectively. To sum up, in the words of Guiguet:

> The conjunction of life and death, the impossibility of love and knowledge, the irremediable loss and the undying presence of the past, form, through a close network of connected and echoing images, a sort of lyrical accompaniment to the whole book.[17]

Desai's style can best be approached from her own statement:

> It is the movement of the wing one tries to capture, not the bird. That is, it is the image that matters.... That is, what a writer's existence is all about—he connects, he connects, all the time he connects. It is a process that does employ language but also transcends it. [18]

Let us examine the following passage from *Cry, the Peacock:*

> Thoughts come, incidents occur, then they are scattered and disappear. Past, present, future, Truth and Untruth. They shuttle back and forth, a shifting chiaroscuro of light and shade, of blood and ashes. (*CTP*, p. 179)

To match the disconnectness of thought and the sudden shifts in perspective, the sentences assume a staccato urgency as if moving in a rush. On the other hand, happier memories of long holidays spent in the hills are savoured in long-winded poetic constructions:

> Better still, my summer home in the hills, in Darjeeling and my little knock-kneed pony that took me for rides ... bearing its load of juice-jammed fruit . . . could not ever end. (*CTP*, p. 78)

While Woolf uses parentheses to ensure the continuity of thought, Desai uses dashes to the same effect:

> He notices a dead branch on one of the silver oaks and, with a small muscle at the corner of his mouth twitching—for he is particular about the garden—he complains of the laziness of the gardener. (*CTP*, p. 39)

The observation is not allowed to be interrupted. hence the discreet insertion about Gautama's preference.

Like Woolf, Desai's prose may also be termed poetic. 'Fall, fall, long fall into the soft velvet wall of the primordium, of original instinct, of first-formed love,' (*CTP*, p. 11) very poetically sums up Maya's longing for love that is the very base of human existence since the very beginning of time. The sentiment is rhythmically summed up in this alliterative passage.

In spite of the above similarities, the styles of Woolf and Desai are different. Woolf's upper class, British style is quite manifest—e.g. in her excessive use of the pronoun "one" which while it appears to withdraw modestly from crude assertion, slyly involves authority from some undefined community of feeling and prejudice, into which it seeks to draw the auditor.'[19] Desai, on the other hand

> is a case of an Indo-Anglian writer who achieves that difficult task of bending the English language to her purpose without either a self-conscious attempt at sounding Indian or seeking the anonymous elegance of public school English.[20]

Writing in an alien tongue, she never considers it a handicap. She, unlike the other Indo-Anglian writers, does not feel the need to incorporate the colloquial flavours into her dialogue for while theirs is an attempt at realism, she, like Woolf, is concerned with the exploration of sensibility.

The vision, in both *Mrs. Dalloway* and *Cry, the Peacock* is undoubtedly tragic. It deals with the terrible isolation of the individual. In *Mrs. Dalloway*, Clarissa, momentarily opts outside the stream of time when she goes into the small empty room while her party is going on. But when she returns to the larger room of human relations, there is a moment of affirmation. It seems as if she has compromised to the existence of mechanical time within which one must operate if one is to transcend time. On the other hand, in *Cry, the Peacock*, Maya hurls herself to death in the manner of Septimus. It is not her final end that signals her option out of the stream of time, but her very insanity that points out to time having no meaning for her. Clarissa, though firmly anchored to her past, is able to adjust to her present, but Maya is totally disoriented with her present and continually escapes to the past. While Clarissa dominates time and memory, Maya is completely dominated by them. From the study of *Mrs. Dalloway* and *Cry, the Peacock*, it is clear that neither Woolf nor Desai believed in the linear, objective course of time. Their perception of time is subjective, coloured as it is, by memory. To quote Lukacs:

> Only in the novel . . . does there occur a creative memory which transfixes the object and transforms it. . . . The duality of inwardness and outside world can here be overcome for the subject 'only when he seeks the . . . unity of his entire life . . . out of the past life-stream which is compressed in memory. . . . The insight which grasps this unity . . . becomes the divinatory-intuitive grasping of the unattained and therefore inexpressible meaning of life. [21]

NOTES

1. Durrell, *Justine* in Higdon, *Time and English Fiction* (London, 1977), p. 107.
2. Gunter Grass, *The Tin Drum*, tr. Ralph Manheim (New York, 1961), p. 17.
3. John Graham, "Time in the Novels of Virginia Woolf" in *Critics on Virginia Woolf*, ed. E.M. Latham (Florida, 1970), p. 29.
4. R. Southwall, "Times Go By Turns."
5. J.H. Raleigh, "The English Novel and the Three Kinds of Times" in *Perspectives in Contemporary Criticism*, ed. S.N. Grebstein (New York, 1965), p. 43.
6. Virginia Woolf, *A Writer's Diary* (London, 1953).
7. Michael Rosenthal, *Virginia Woolf* (London, 1979), p. 90.
8. Ralph Freedman, *The Lyrical Novel* (New Jersey, 1966), p. 186.
9. *A Writer's Diary*, p. 60.
10. Ibid., p. 61.

11. Ibid., p. 52.

12. Joan Bennett, *Virginia Woolf: Her Art as a Novelist* (Cambridge, 1964), p. 79.

13. Robin Majumdar and Allen McLaurin, ed., *Virginia Woolf: The Critical Heritage* (London, 1975), p. 17.

14. Irene Simon, "Some Images in *Mrs. Dalloway*" in Latham, p. 59.

15. David Lodge, "Some Verbal Features of Virginia Woolf's Novels" in Latham, p. 26.

16. Ibid.

17. J. Guiguet, *Virginia Woolf and Her Works* (London, 1965), p. 452.

18. Anita Desai, "The Indian Writer's Problems," *Language Forum*, Vol. 7 Nos. 1-4, April 1981-March 1982, p. 226.

19. Lodge in Latham, p. 26.

20. Meenakshi Mukherjee, *The Twice-Born Fiction* (New Delhi, 1971), p. 40.

21. Georg Lukacs, *The Theory of the Novel* (London, 1978), p. 122.

TO THE LIGHTHOUSE and *CLEAR LIGHT OF DAY*

> Everything goes, everything returns, the wheel of existence rolls for ever. Everything dies, everything blossoms anew, the year of existence runs on for ever.
>
> Nietzsche

Virginia Woolf's estimate of *To the Lighthouse*, on its completion in 1926 reads—'it is easily the best of my books'[1]—an opinion shared even by her most confirmed detractors, notable among them being F.R. Leavis, who attributed the success of the book to its autobiographical bias. The Hebrides Isles in *To the Lighthouse*, do in fact call to mind the island of St. Ives in Cornwall, the setting of Woolf's childhood. Memory is the motivating force behind the germination of the novel. As Woolf herself confirms:

> This is going to be fairly short, to have father's character done complete in it; and mother's; and St. Ives and childhood and all the usual things I try to put in—life, death etc.[2]

While the novel was an artistically satisfying achievement for Woolf, it was also an exercise in exorcising the ghosts of her dead parents. On the ninety sixth anniversary of her father's birth, she wrote 'I used to think of him and mother daily; but writing *The Lighthouse* laid them in my mind.'[3]

While *To the Lighthouse* was Woolf's fifth novel, *Clear Light of Day* is Desai's sixth and likewise considered the best of her works to date. Desai's *Where Shall We Go This Summer ?* closely resembles *To the Lighthouse* in having an island setting, a father image and division into three sections, among other parallels, but, in range, depth and sensitivity, it is *Clear Light of Day* that comes closest to *To the Lighthouse*. In *Where Shall We Go This Summer ?*, we have the hysterical responses of the hypersensitive Sita that jar on the nerves. She seems the comfortably placed wife looking for diversion and it is Raman who enlists reader sympathy. With a display of great intensity, she goes to Manori, trying to live vicariously her favourite poem by Cavafy, but when she meekly and almost thankfully follows Raman back to Bombay, the book ends in a whimper. *Clear Light of Day*, a nomination for the prized Booker award has all the ingredients of a gripping novel—it is sensitive, carefully constructed and beautifully written with subtle touches of humour. Desai takes the 1947 partition as the central episode but does not appropriate it thematically as do some other Indo-Anglian writers. Though she nowhere indicates *Clear Light of Day* to be autobiographical, we definitely get a glimpse into her own experiences from her sensitive and vivid portrayal of childhood.

Ralph Freedman calls *To the Lighthouse* "a novel of manners" depicting the upper middle class academic society in Edwardian England. He feels that the novel has a conventional plot. But the way time is treated here would suggest otherwise. As Erich Auerbach puts it, we feel as if events were "cut loose from the present of the exterior circumstances and range freely through the depths of time.'[4] The shape here again is polytemporal with "psychological" time obtruding constantly and breaking all chronological sequence, though on the surface, the action completes itself in the course of one day—the evening and morning being separated by a long night of ten years. In *Clear Light of Day*, the main event in focus is the partition but it is clear that Desai is not interested in mere chronology, but 'in discovering the final pattern of meaning that emerges out of the apparent meaninglessness of life in a small family.'[5] This she achieves by using Time as 'an elastic medium, capable of expanding according to the emotional "breadth" of the moment.'[6]

While in *Mrs. Dalloway*, Woolf has completely waived the convention of demarcating her narrative into chapters, we find *To the Lighthouse*, divided into three precise parts. In Part I, Woolf delves into a moment in time in all its minute factual detail. In Part II, she "races through ten faceless years" within a space of twenty pages, and in Part III 'she descends again to the plane of human time and fact to explore the details of that second moment.'[7] "The Window" which is the title given to Part I, has been interpreted by John Graham as an image associated 'with the individual's vision of life; "Time Passes" portrays the assault of time on the integrity of the vision; and in the third, "The Lighthouse," the vision is triumphantly reaffirmed.'[8] It would seem as if Time is handled in a manner similar to that in *Mrs. Dalloway* because we still have Woolf operating within the framework of a single day, yet here is a difference for 'the author sometimes confuses the order of events in a most ingenious manner.'[9]

Clear Light of Day is divided into four untitled parts. Though there is an apparently chaotic shift in perspective from past to present, there actually is perfect harmony as in an exquisitely composed musical composition. Jameson discussing Lukacs' views on the modern novel talks of how in it time becomes 'profoundly ambiguous in nature, a force both life-giving and life-destroying.'[10] Desai too, feels that her novel is about 'time as a destroyer, as a preserver and about what the bondage of time does to people.'[11] The link with the philosophy of the *Four Quartets* is unmistakable. 'The four sections of the novel, suggesting the "four dimensions" of time record the transitions that take place in a New Delhi family.'[12] Part I opens with the koels providing a lyrical background to Tara's musings. Bim's reminiscences of her childhood take up most of Part II while Part III is given over to Tara's point of view. The final section is shared by the two sisters and is rounded off with Bim who roving 'from note to note, searching for harmony, experimenting with sequences' (*CLD*, p. 179) realises in a moment of vision that 'Time the destroyer, is time the preserver.' (*CLD*, p. 182) It is somewhat similar to Lily Briscoe's moment of vision at the end of *To the Lighthouse*, when, with a flourish, she completes the painting.

In both *Clear Light of Day* and *To the Lighthouse*, we have the three fold effect of time—'the passing of moments or hours, the voyage from youth to age, and the historical time, or time in relation to nation-wide events.'[13] In Woolf, inner time is not in contradistinction to outer time, for she decried the isolation of the Self (a defect she finds in Joyce). To her, the external and the internal are complementary. Both Woolf and Desai use inner time without ignoring its relation to the outer. In *Clear Light of Day*, the passing of moments is exemplified by the description of Tara's first morning in Delhi. Through the reminiscences of Tara and Bim, we are taken to their childhood and made aware of their growing up to youth and then to middle age. We are also made to see how Time affects the course of nations. Instead of celebrating the achievement of independence, Desai laments the partition, not because of its political implications, but for the bloodshed and insane prejudice that followed in its wake. Similarly in *To the Lighthouse*, moments tick by as Mrs. Ramsay sits with

James cutting up pictures from the illustrated catalogue. The passage of years is depicted as James and the younger Ramsay children grow up into adolescence and finally, we are told of the war raging in Europe, deciding the fate of nations and of individuals. For instance, the Ramsay family is affected by the death of Andrew, the most brilliant of the Ramsay children.

In both *Clear Light of Day* and *To the Lighthouse*, though mind time and linear time are depicted side by side, the final triumph is reserved for "mind time" or durée. Just as Big Ben marks the passage of time in *Mrs. Dalloway*, in *To the Lighthouse* it is the changing light in the garden that indicates the flow of time. "Time Passes," which merges the night with the passage of ten years, has Time playing havoc with men and material, resulting in the deaths of Mrs. Ramsay, Prue and Andrews and leading to the dilapidation of the Ramsay house. Though Time the destroyer reigns supreme here, the final section shows the triumph of Time the Preserver over Time the Destroyer. For even though Mrs. Ramsay is dead, the memory of her helps materialise the long planned trip to the Lighthouse and also results in Lily Briscoe's vision. In *Clear Light of Day*, Time the Destroyer apparently seems triumphant as it leaves a trail of deaths in the Das household but when Bim corroborates Tara's statement 'Nothing's over, ever,' (*CLD*, p. 173) we are made aware of the cyclic nature of things—and though dead long ago, the Das parents, Mira Masi and the Hyder Alis continue to haunt the pages with a presence that smacks of permanence even within a swiftly changing world. This is possible only through memory, used in a way reminiscent of Proust's method.

The main theme of *Clear Light of Day* is time as both the destroyer and the preserver. This is best exemplified in the last episode when both Mulk and his ageing guru are to sing at a *soirée* to which Bim and Tara have also been invited. Though both belong to the same school of singing, Mulk's voice is 'rich, dark, while the guru, once a famous singer can only sing in a small, ancient voice . . . rough-edged and raw as if in pain.' (*CLD*, p. 181) Writes Desai:

> The contrast between Mulk's voice and his was great: whereas Mulk's voice had been almost like a child's, so sweet and clear, or a young man's full and ripe and with a touch of sweetness to it, the old man's was sharp, even a little cracked, inclined to break,

> although not merely with age but with the bitterness of his experiences, the sadness and passion and frustration. (*CLD*, pp. 181-182)

Bimla realises that Time that had destroyed the talent in one had nurtured it in the other and thus the torch of life was handed down from one generation to the next. In the "Time Passes" section of *To the Lighthouse*, the same theme can be discerned. While the Ramsay's summer house is about to succumb to the vagaries of time, it is Mrs. McNab, an old woman with a duster in her hand, reminiscent of the figure of Time with the scythe, who paradoxically, wages a battle against Time and manages to restore and repair the havoc played by it.

Time does not deal the same fate to everyone. In *To the Lighthouse*, Time disrupts the family happiness of the Ramsays by snatching away Mrs. Ramsay, Prue and Andrew. It has also not been kind to the Rayleys. The love once shared so ardently by Paul and Minta has disintegrated with the passage of time. Mr. Ramsay, who symbolises his intellectual achievements by the letters of the alphabet is stuck at the letter "Q." On the other hand, Time is bountiful to Carmichael, who finds himself a famous poet in his old age. In *Clear Light of Day*, Time has a different fate in store for Raja and Bim than the one they had ordained for themselves. Childhood dreams of becoming a hero and a heroine are swamped in the mire of circumstance. The would-be hero finds himself playing the role of a fat, prosperous *pasha* indulging his hobby, but with no vocation to follow. Bim becomes nothing more spectacular than a college lecturer. Though she cannot become a Joan of Arc, at least she is able to wrest some heroism out of her existence by managing single-handed her troublesome family. One would have least expected Tara, the baby of the family, to achieve her ambition. Her pompous childhood declaration of 'I am going to be a mother and knit for my babies' (*CLD*, p. 112) proves true. Comparing the fates of Bim and Tara, one is reminded of Browning:

> That low man seeks a little thing to do,
> Sees it and does it . . .
> This high man, aiming at a million,
> Misses an unit. ("The Grammarian's Funeral")

It would be interesting to note that of all the women in Desai's fiction, Tara comes closest to the concept of a happily married woman. Maya, Sita, Nanda Kaul and Monisha all seem actively frustrated. Their sense of alienation seems to be a pointer to Desai's own ambivalent attitude towards marriage.

Both *To the Lighthouse* and *Clear Light of Day* deal with death, the death of loved ones and 'the death of a beloved place and time.'[14] The passage of time results in loneliness and isolation for some, as with Lily and Bim. It is as if the theme of loneliness is being carried over from the earlier novels, *Mrs. Dalloway* and *Cry, the Peacock.* But instead of ending on a note of fatality, both *To the Lighthouse* and *Clear Light of Day* end in affirmation, with Lily having her vision and Bim reconciling to the change that she had hitherto violently rejected (that of Raja breaking away from the family fold), so that 'like matches struck in the dark,'[15] the reader is enlightened as he glimpses fleetingly into what Woolf calls "lifc itsclf."

In both *Clear Light of Day* and *To the Lighthouse*, we have the Proustian phenomenon of memory transcending time itself. Mrs. Ramsay lives on long after her death and so does Mira *masi*. Human consciousness breaks away the limits imposed by time. To recall Raja's favourite verse from Iqbal:

> Thou didst create night but I made the lamp
> Thou didst create clay but I made the cup
> . . . It is I who made the glass out of stone
> And it is I who turn a poison into an antidote.
>
> (*CLD*, p. 50)

Here, it is obvious that man is able to wrest some heroism out of his momentary existence. In *To the Lighthouse*, when Nancy Ramsay plays on the seashore, she creates an imaginary world by placing her hand on the puddle:

> She changed the pool into the sea, and made the minnows into sharks and whales, and cast vast clouds over this tiny world by holding her hand against the sun, and so brought darkness and desolation, like God Himself. . . . (*TTL*, p. 87)

But when she sees the vast sea before her and the little puddle where she has been playing, she is struck by the contrast and the feeling of the Nothingness of human life. All the same, she has had her moment of creativity and supremacy.

In *Clear Light of Day* we are presented with the paradox of change and continuity. Tara returns to her childhood home after years abroad and asks 'Why had nothing changed ? She had changed—why did it not keep up with her.' (*CLD*, p. 12) Similarly, in *To the Lighthouse*, Lily thinks, 'There is a coherence in things, a stability, something, she meant is immune from change and shines out (. . .) in the face of the flowing, the fleeting, the spectral, like a ruby.' (*TTL*, p. 121) In *Clear Light of Day*, much as Tara feels that she has changed, it is evident that she has not lost her childhood fascination for snails (a fascination, she incidentally, shares with Neville in *The Waves*) and her penchant for hard astringent guavas. At heart, she is still the same shy Tara. But Time brings change as well. Tara tells Bim, 'no one could have ever believed that you and Raja who were so close—so close—could be against each other ever.' (*CLD*, pp. 28-29) Bim continues to nurse her grudge against Raja to the very end. In both the novels, the characters tend to eulogize the past in contrast to the present. In *Clear Light of Day*, 'It seemed to Tara that there had been far more roses in it when she was a child' as she strolls down the rose walk of their shabby house. Mrs. Ramsay in *To the Lighthouse*, while passing by an artist cannot help observing how in her grandmother's day people were far more meticulous and "took the greatest pains." Mrs. McNab, unwinding "her ball of memories" remembers the past and thinks 'Things were better then than now.' (*TTL*, p. 156)

Sharing something for even a moment binds one to the chain of time. Of Mrs. Ramsay's *boeuf en daube* dinner, Marder tells us that 'the dinner has been eaten, has disappeared, but something permanent remains, a creation that partakes of eternity.'[16] When Bim realises that the soil of her house 'contained all time, past and future in it. . . . It was where her deepest self lived, and the deepest selves of her sister and brothers and all those who shared that time with her,' (*CLD*, p. 182) she is able to forgive and forget. No amount of rancour can corrode the tenacious ties that she shares with her family.

Both Woolf and Desai take us to the "submerged selves" of their characters. In *To the Lighthouse*, we have Lily also expressing Woolf's oft-repeated opinion about the difficulty of really knowing anyone:

> ... this making up scenes about them, is what we call, 'knowing people,' 'thinking of them,' 'being fond' of them ! Not a word of it was true, she had made it up, but it was what she knew them by all the same. (*TTL*, p. 196)

Both authors aim to achieve a multidimensional effect in character and the method employed is that of reflection and memory. Lily's reflections about Mrs. Ramsay indicate not only what she thought of her but also what William Bankes felt about her. 'She was astonishingly beautiful, William said,' (*TTL*, p. 201) a fact reiterated by Tansley and the others. But Lily personally feels 'But beauty was not everything.... It stilled life—fröze it.' (*TTL*, pp. 201-202) In *Clear Light of Day*, Bim is described in Tara's reflection as 'Bim, grey and heavy now and not so unlike their mother in appearance, only awake, watchful, gazing at her with her fullest attention and appraisal.' (*CLD*, p. 2)

Mrs. Woolf felt that personality is not a homogeneous entity but is rather made up of moments of experience, for example, when Lily searches time for her memories of Mrs. Ramsay, she encounters a "fresh memory" displaying a different Mrs. Ramsay. Here there is no "integrated self" but at least there is a "key self" which is "able to call up the other selves," which are linked through the threads of memory, sensory stimulus or association.'[17] Hence Mrs. Ramsay's "key self" is that of a life-giver for 'the whole of the effort of merging and flowing and creating rested on her.' (*TTL*, p. 96) And to this self are associated her other faces—those of an incorrigible matchmaker, a social worker, a selfish mother whose 'own daughter must be happier than other people's daughters.' (*TTL*, p. 126) Hence association and memory help in piecing together the separate aspects of a character, giving the reader an insight into the very essence of that character. Though we are not told Mrs. Ramsay's Christian name (her dignity does not encourage familiarity) yet she is a memorable character, an archetype of the eternal mother. Mrs. Woolf generally gives her characters an alter ego in another character. In *Mrs. Dalloway*, Septimus is the double of Clarissa. In *To the Lighthouse* it is Lily Briscoe whose arid and somewhat sexless nature complements the creative aspect of Mrs. Ramsay and the two units to form an "integrated self." In *Clear Light of Day*, the characters' ruminations highlight certain events while others are lost to memory and this in turn reveals their traits. Tara cannot forget her desertion of Bim when attacked by bees. This is only a prelude to her final desertion—her marriage to Bakul and escape from family responsibilities. Bim remembers her own role as the mother figure in a family of ailing aunt and brother and how she nurses them selflessly. Here she is like Mrs. Ramsay who "makes of the moment something permanent." She has a creative streak like Mrs. Ramsay, a somewhat masculine, sexless nature like Lily Briscoe. In fact, she seems to fit Coleridge's definition that "a great mind is androgynous" and becomes an integrated self when she has her final vision.

Mr. and Mrs. Ramsay's attitudes to time help demonstrate the basic difference in their natures. Mrs. Ramsay looks into the garden and by the changing light is able to guess the time. On the other hand, when Mr. Ramsay wants to know if it is getting late, he 'flicked his watch carelessly open. But it was only just past seven.' (*TTL*, p. 78) While Mrs. Ramsay's knowledge is intuitive and immediate, his is factual and theoretical. In *Clear Light of Day*, it is Bakul who like Mr. Ramsay is governed by the precise ticking of the clock. He tells Tara 'The car will be here any minute and you know uncle is very punctual. We mustn't keep him waiting.' (*CLD*, p. 17) Tara, on the other hand, in spite of her husband's careful grooming, goes back to being the 'languid little girl, listless, a dawdler, (*CLD*, p. 10) in the "hopeless atmosphere" of her childhood home.

Richter points out that Woolf adds an extra-dimension to some characters by investing them with mythical significance and thus 'projecting it into times and prehistory and endowing it with an emotional area deriving mainly from a level below that of personal memory.'[18] The reference to myth places the narrative in a world above or prior to ordinary time, *in illo tempore* as Mircea Eliade would put it. In *To the Lighthouse*, Woolf describes Carmichael 'looking like an old pagan God, shaggy, with weeds in his hair and the trident (it was only a French novel) in his hand, (*TTL*, p. 236) and here the reference to Shiva is obvious. It is further strengthened when Lily continues 'He stood there spreading his hands over all the weakness and suffering of mankind, she thought he was surveying, tolerantly, compassionately their final destiny.' (*TTL*, p. 237) In *Clear Light of Day*, when Bim experiences a momentary upsurge of incestuous feelings for Baba, she finds him 'unresponsive as a god, guilt-arousing as a saint.' (*CLD*, p. 167) So Baba can no longer be simply dismissed as a retarded individual but an enigma that is as inscrutable as his silences.

Meenakshi Mukherjee says that 'theme is not something that can be examined separately from the technique of a novel because the theme is determined by the novelist's choice of point of view.'[19] In both *Clear Light of Day* and *To the Lighthouse*, the point of view is shifting. In *To the Lighthouse*, the reader is led in and out of the minds of Mrs. Ramsay, Lily Briscoe, Tansley, Bankes, Ramsay, Mrs. McNab with the omniscient narrator never far away. But most of the events are filtered through the consciousness and Mrs. Ramsay and Lily Briscoe. As the emphasis is placed on the reflections of these female characters, it is easy to see why the writer resorts to nostalgia. In *Clear Light of Day*, apart from the omniscient narrator, we are turned over to the thoughts of Tara and Bim—both female characters again and given to nostalgia which Desai makes sure does not disintegrate into sentimentality. And the constant shift from past to present, is reminiscent of the oral tradition of story-telling. The story-teller remembers his own experiences at random and communicates them in a meandering, repetitive style. This style is also part of the literary tradition of India and one used in the *Mahabharatha* and the *Ramayana*. Walter Benjamin in *Illuminations* says that behind every story there is a moral to which the novelist's answer would be that his aim is to convey through his medium the meaning of life. Hence, in Desai's style, we have a flavour of the ancient *raconteur*.

In *To the Lighthouse*, the theme of solitude, death and memory goes as well with the background of the sea that J.H. Roberts says 'As to the problem of form, *To the Lighthouse* structurally is like a pool which narcissistically reflects its theme. . . .'[20] Similarly, the four parts of *Clear Light of Day* are like the four instruments being played in perfect harmony in a quartet. Just like a refrain, there is repetition of certain episodes in both *To the Lighthouse* and *Clear Light of Day*. According to Zola, the uses of repetition are unity and intensification. But repetition:

> also helps the writer to achieve a Proustian fusion of past and present when the reader is reminded by image, phrase and allusion of prior events. Past and present are in this way linked together in the reader's mind.[21]

Baba's discordant record-playing on the ancient HMV gramophone punctuates most reveries throughout *Clear Light of Day*. This outdated contraption, salvaged from Hyder Ali's house, becomes a voice from the past that runs parallel to the character's consciousness of the present.

In *To the Lighthouse*, the mention of the proposed expedition to the lighthouse recurs throughout the book and becomes the binding factor not only of the narrative, but also links the living to the dead. Mrs. Ramsay's wish is fulfilled after death and Mr. Ramsay is thus able to redeem his promise to his wife and to realise himself as he steps outside the confines of his ego 'on to the rock' (*TTL*, p. 236) of self-awareness.

Proust regarded involuntary memory as more important than voluntary memory which is apt to be governed by the intellect. On the other hand, involuntary memory is evoked by visual, verbal tactile or nasal associations. In *To the Lighthouse*, on the way to the lighthouse, James Ramsay reacts to the visual stimulus of his sister Cam who reminds him of his mother. This remembrance once again ignites the hatred for his father that dates back to his early childhood when he was shattered by his father's repeated pessimistic pronouncements regarding the impossibility of the trip to the lighthouse. In *Clear Light of Day*, the sight of the river takes the sisters back to their childhood games played on the sand dunes and the mosaic of memories is filled with images of Raja the adoring boy watching the grand Hyder Ali on his white horse. This in turn leads Bim to the memory of the objectionable letter Raja had written years ago and one she had harboured like a thorn in her flesh. To sum up in Richter's words:

> Not only is the past always with us, but consciousness is forever changing, and so our memories, redefined each moment by the present self and coloured by fresh perceptions, are in a state of continuous alteration. By presenting the initial stimulus, the character's successive memories of it are revived, the sense of internal change and motion which we feel as living or growing older, can be expressed.[22]

The person remembering a childhood incident at twenty is different from the same person remembering the same incident at forty. Therefore, it is clear that memory alters with experience and age. Bim is able to purge herself of the intense hatred that she felt for Raja for with time she realises 'No other love had started so far back in time and had had so much time in which to grow and spread' (*CLD*, p. 165) than that she felt for her family. Similarly, in *To the Lighthouse*, at the slightest praise from his father, James is able to shed his resentment that had once been so intense in childhood.

In *To the Lighthouse*, there is a wilful confusion of the time sequence and it would require an exceptionally attentive reader to keep pace with the changes. From page 5 to page 12, we have Mrs. Ramsay sitting with James; pages 12-18 relate the expedition to town with Tansley and page 18 brings us back to the window and the process of James cutting pictures from an illustrated catalogue. In between, we also have references to dinner and the children 'disappearing as stealthily as stags' (*TTL*, p. 11) to criticise Charles Tansley. Only a careful reading would indicate that the trip to town had taken place before the opening scene of the novel. It is not presented from Mrs. Ramsay's viewpoint but the author has deliberately altered the time sequence, not to confuse, but to achieve an amorphous effect, like wave merging into wave. The viewpoint is constantly shifting—as the event of landing at the lighthouse is viewed differently by Lily on the shore and the Ramsay children on the island. But unity is maintained throughout by the narrator's voice that regulates the prose.

In *Clear Light of Day*, the narrator's voice dominates. In *To the Lighthouse*, it is easy to follow the transition from one character's thoughts to the other, but at times the narrator's voice becomes so discreet that it melts with the character's. In the following passage from *Clear Light of Day*, in response to Bim's query whether she could sleep:

> 'How could I ?' cried Tara, laughing, and talked of the koels in the morning, and the dog barking in the night, and the mosquitoes singing and stinging in the dark. . . . Tara in her elegant pale blue nightgown . . . and Bim in a curious shapeless hand-made garment. . . . At the feet a border of blue and green peacocks redeemed the dress from total shabbiness and was—Tara laughed lightly—original. 'How he barks,' she repeated. 'Don't the neighbours complain ?' (*CLD*, p. 3)

The sentences are undoubtedly the narrator's but the underlined sentence could either be the narrator's observation or Tara's thoughts and here the distinction between the two seems to melt.

In *To the Lighthouse*, the "Time Passes" section has been variously criticised as a superimposition, out of time with the rest of the book.

Its best defence comes in the words of Schaefer, 'In context, Part II performs an important technical function, giving the reader space in which to allow experience to change into memory by the alchemy of time.'[23] In this section, most factual details are reported within parentheses. But the parentheses are not only used for conveying remarks by the narrator but also for indicating the shifts in the character's thoughts. In *Clear Light of Day*, the book opens at the present moment with the *koels* announcing day-break. The *koels* are present throughout, signalling the passage of time. 'In the garden, *a koel* lifted itself out of the heavy torpor of the afternoon and called tentatively, as if enquiring into the existence of the evening.' (*CLD*, p. 166) Not only the *koels* but

> it was the sound of the house, as much as the contented muttering of the pigeons in the verandah. It gave time a continuity and regularity that the ticking of a clock in the hall might convey in other houses. (*CLD*, p. 102)

In Desai, the house becomes a motif in the structure of the novel. It is a focal point to which the characters' thoughts are inextricably bound—Carignano in *Fire on the Mountain*, the old crumbling mansion in *Clear Light of Day* and in *Cry, the Peacock* the large house in Lucknow. Lucknow or New Delhi or Kasauli thus represent a nostalgic longing for days gone by even if in some cases the past way of life is rejected for example, in *Clear Light of Day* Tara has consciously broken away from the life that she is nostalgic for.

When Tara revisits her old home, she is reminded of the past at every juncture. Part II deals with the partition days while Part III takes us even further back to the childhood of the Das children. Part IV brings the reader back to the present, which is again loaded with memories of the past. In the words of John M. Gregory, 'Memory is the central set piece of the novel and remembering and enduring are the inexorable activities of the Das family.'[24]

Some of the similarities between *To the Lighthouse* and *Clear Light of Day* may strike one as superficial but the major point of convergence of both these novels is memory. In *To the Lighthouse*, the lighthouse is a symbol of eternity in the midst of the changing waves; in *Clear Light of Day*, it is the old Das house, steeped in memories that stands as a staid bulwark in the turbulent lives of the characters in a world of swiftly-changing values. Both Woolf and Desai have stressed the importance of the heart over the head, emotion over calculation. For *'L' intelligence ne peut trouver le temps perdu.'*[25]

NOTES

1. Virginia Woolf, *A Writer's Diary* (London, 1953), p. 102.
2. Ibid., pp. 76-77.
3. Ibid., p. 138.
4. E. Auerbach quoted in J. Naremore, *The World Without A Self* (New Haven, 1973), p. 113.
5. R.S. Sharma, *Anita Desai* (New Delhi, 1981), p. 130.
6. L. Ruddick, *The Seen and the Unseen* (Cambridge, 1977), p. 14.
7. Ibid., p. 20.
8. J. Graham, "Time in the Novels of Virginia Woolf," *Critics on Virginia Woolf*, ed. Latham (Florida, 1970), p. 33.
9. Naremore, p. 113.
10. F. Jameson, *Marxism and Form* (New Jersey, 1971), pp. 176-177.
11. Interview with Anita Desai, *India Today*, Dec. 1-15, 1980, p. 142.
12. Sharma, p. 132.
13. Joan Bennett, *Virginia Woolf: Her Art as a Novelist* (Cambridge, 1964), p. 98.
14. Naremore, p. 112.
15. Virginia Woolf, *A Writer's Diary*.
16. Marder, *Feminism and Art* (Chicago, 1968), p. 45.
17. H. Richter, *Virginia Woolf: The Inward Voyage* (New Jersey, 1978), p. 117.
18. Ibid., p. 123.
19. Meenakshi Mukherjee, *The Twice-Born Fiction* (New Delhi, 1971), p. 37.
20. J.H. Roberts, "Vision and Design" in Latham, p. 69.
21. A. McLaurin, *Virginia Woolf: The Echoes Enslaved* (Cambridge, 1973), p. 101.
22. Richter.

23. J. Schaefer, "Mr and Mrs Ramsay" in Latham, p. 73.

24. J.M. Gregory, Book Review of *Clear Light of Day*, *Commonwealth Novel in English*, Vol. I, No.1, Jan. 1982, p. 110.

25. Proust, quoted in R. Ironside, "The Artistic Vision of Proust," *Horizon* , Vol. IV, No.19, July 1941, p. 37.

THE WAVES and *FIRE ON THE MOUNTAIN*

Men's curiosity searches past and future
And clings to that dimension. But to apprehend
The point of intersection of the timeless
With Time, is an occupation for the saint. . . .

T.S. Eliot

At first glance, it would seem that no two books could be more dissimilar than *The Waves* and *Fire on the Mountain*. While *Fire on the Mountain* is a novel in the conventional sense of the word, *The Waves* is more of a 'serious, mystical poetical work'[1] than a novel, as the term is conventionally understood. Both Woolf and Desai have taken recourse to highly disparate techniques and it is only in some thematic aspects that points of convergence can be discerned. *The Waves* is Mrs. Woolf's seventh novel while *Fire on the Mountain* ranks fifth in the works of a still-developing author. While in *Fire on the Mountain*, Desai is in a mellow ruminative mood, in *The Waves* Woolf is at her most innovative, manipulating words and phrases in a manner aimed at engaging the reader in a unique literary experience.

Woolf conceived *The Waves* as 'a new kind of play, prose yet poetry, a novel and a play.'[2] Even though the italicised paragraphs at the head of the sections seem to suggest 'stage directions,'[3] and though the speeches of the six major characters are enclosed within inverted commas, the book cannot be called a play, for the characters are not conversing with one another but merely speaking. At best it can be called the play-poem that Woolf longed to write. In 1926, before *The Waves* took shape, Woolf wrote in her diary that she was

> haunted by the notion of a novel about the life of a woman in which all shall be told on one occasion; and time shall be obliterated. . . . My theory being that the actual event does not exist—nor time either.[4]

Hence time, as measured by clocks, is totally subservient to the "moment" which includes 'the external framework of consecutive time and the individual's internal journeys into past, present and future.'[5] And it is the "moment" which is the symbol of time for Woolf, a symbol of the "here and now" that she strives to express. 'To begin with: the present moment is largely composed of visual and sense impressions,'[6] and the expression of this dictates the technique of *The Waves* which makes frequent use of "I see," "Look," "I hear," in order to fling a "myriad impressions" on the reader's psyche.

Rather than wanting to produce a 'mystical, eyeless book,'[7] Anita Desai deals with the isolation in the lives of her three characters Nanda Kaul, Raka and Ila Das. Though not a traditional story, *Fire on the Mountain* is rooted in a particular time and space, while *The Waves* is let adrift the stream of eternity. Desai explores the reality around her and tries to

> discover its significance by plunging below the surface and plumbing the depths, then illuminating those depths till they become a more lucid, brilliant and explicable reflection of the visible world.[8]

Like *Mrs. Dalloway*, *To the Lighthouse* and *Between the Acts*, *The Waves* is held together within the framework of a single day. While in *Mrs. Dalloway* it is Big Ben that tolls the passing of hours, in *To the Lighthouse* it is the changing light in the garden and in *The Waves* it is the journey of the sun across the sky that signals the passage of the day. But time here, goes beyond seasons and human lives, thus entering a timeless universe where particular lives merge into existence in general. The forward movement of time as the characters move from childhood, youth to old age is stemmed in Bernard's summing-up when the reel of time past is unwound. The frequent hints about the recurrence of time, 'the incessant rise and fall and rise again' (*TW*, p. 200) of the waves suggest cosmic time. 'Nietzsche and Woolf both cultivate the "Eternal Moment" where Past and Future intersect.'[9] For instance, Bernard while relating childhood experiences says 'All these things happen in one second and last forever.' (*TW*, p. 162) The present moment exists but it is too elusive to be grasped. It is only in moments of intensity that Time stands still while the world moves on as in the case of Percival's dinner.

In *Fire on the Mountain*, the narrative completes itself in a few summer days in the small Himalayan town Kasauli. But in this short period, the entire panorama of the lives of the protagonists unfolds itself either in the authorial voice or in the musings of the characters themselves. Time does not flow in a forward sequential movement but there are constant references to the past.

> Nanda Kaul unconsciously seeks to freeze Time into a motionless constancy, but Time keeps moving through her past which she recapitulates as she reacts to her present surroundings.[10]

Hence, inner time flows independently of clock time but it is not rooted entirely in the self for its existence depends upon the stimuli from the external world of objects and images.

The Waves has nine sections of varying lengths, each preceded by an italicised passage that lyrically weaves in the images of the sun, the sea and the song of the birds. These italicised descriptions of nature represent the impersonal macrocosm against which the microcosm of the individual lives is held in tension, in the intervening dramatic passages. Like the four stages in the life of man in Shakespeare, Woolf depicts nine here, each stage coinciding with the rising of the sun to its decline and disappearance. The book begins on the note 'The sun had not yet risen" (*TW*, p. 5) and this position of the sun is parallel to childhood when the six protagonists relate their perception of the world around them in picturesque single sentences. The sun rises higher and we find the children in school and college and when it reaches its zenith, we are told of Percival's death. Thence begins the decline and it touches its nadir at Bernard's summing-up when he recounts the story of his life to a hypothetical listener, a stranger who seems more a figment of Bernard's imagination than a real person.

Fire on the Mountain is divided into three sections each neatly dealing with a specific event. Part I has Nanda Kaul hovering between past and present when the future obtrudes in the shape of a letter announcing the impending arrival of an unwanted great-grandchild. Part II, the longest, is composed of twenty-one chapters and is devoted to Raka's arrival and sojourn at Carignano. Here, Desai, very subtly, depicts the change in Nanda Kaul's attitude to Raka. We see Nanda Kaul changing from sheer hostility to indifference to acceptance, to admiration and finally to affection for her little visitor. Part III, which describes in some detail the visit of Ila Das, a childhood friend of Nanda Kaul, also consists of the denouement and may be rightly considered a masterly piece of construction. The strands of the two lives of Ila and Nanda Kaul which had run parallel since the very beginning, converging at certain points, are finally tied in the knot of death. And we have the archetypal fire of cremation when:

> Down in the ravine, the flames spat and crackled around the dry wood and through the dry grass, and black smoke spiralled up over the mountain. (*FOM*, p. 146)

It is significant to note that Part III ends in thirteen chapters, the numeral having superstitious connotations of doom and disaster.

While inner time helps human beings transcend the limits of the flesh, it is in clock time itself that events unfold themselves. It is in time that the protagonists in *The Waves* grow up and it is time that brings death and decay. Jinny, who can easily summon a stranger to her side because of her physical charms, feels her power waning with advancing age. She realises 'I shall look into faces and I shall see them seek some other face.' (*TW*, p. 131) It is interesting to note that while the characters change, there is no change as Rhoda says 'There is, then, a world immune from change.' (*TW*, p. 72) Jinny remains the sensuous siren, Rhoda the shy misanthrope, Bernard, the phrase-maker, Susan the mother figure. But the change is perceptible, however subtle it might be. Susan, who in earlier days, would rise with the lark submits to the placidity of maternity and age saying "But I never rise at dawn and see the purple drops in the cabbage leaves. . . ."(*TW*, p. 116) The characters react differently to sensations with the change in age. When Mrs. Constable squeezes the sponge on his back, Bernard reacts by saying "Bright arrows of sensation shoot on either side." (*TW*, p. 18) And in old age, recalling the incident, he muses:

> And so, as long as we drew breath, for the rest of time, if we knock against a chair, a table, or a woman, we are pierced with arrows of sensation—if we walk in a garden, if we drink this wine. (*TW*, p. 162)

Hence from this philosophising, we realise that Bernard the child is now a man.

In *Fire on the Mountain*, Time has been unkind to all the characters. Nanda Kaul has spent her life doing what duty demanded and the futility of her imposed role leaves her cynical and embittered. At a fairly advanced age, she is released from the bondage of playing the Vice-Chancellor's busy wife and so it is with vengeance that she opts for a life of complete stagnation. However, in the final pages we realise that even now she had no choice. 'She did not live here alone by choice—she lived here alone because that was what she was forced to do, reduced to doing.' (*FOM*, p. 145) Raka, we are told 'was a recluse by nature, by instinct.' (*FOM*, p. 48) But this is not true for when we study her reactions to the wild revelries at the club, we know that her withdrawal into herself has been occasioned by the memory of a drunken father beating a cringing mother. Ila Das, born in an aristocratic family, is reduced by time and circumstance to such a state of poverty that she cannot buy even half a kilo of cornmeal. Her problems are clearly financial thus giving the lie to B. Ramachandra Rao's generalization that 'Their [the characters of Desai] problems are psychological or spiritual, not social or economical.'[11] In *Fire on the Mountain*, the disparity of the perceptions of childhood and age are depicted in Nanda Kaul's awareness of the "barrenness and stillness" of the life around her, while Raka is alive to the infinity of movement and the variety of life around her:

> She patted a child of wood here, smoothed a ridge of plaster there. She met a spider that groomed its hairs in a corner, saw lizards' eyes blinking out of a dark groove. (*FOM*, p. 41)

With the passage of time, events and memories lose their intensity. In *The Waves*, the death of Percival shocks all the characters with a shattering impact, but, as time passes Rhoda admits, voicing the feelings of the others. 'I seldom think of Percival now' (*TW*, p. 139) when at the first shock of his death Neville had exclaimed, 'The lights of the world have gone out.' (*TW*, p. 101) Though time may blunt the edge of pain it cannot obliterate memories, for Percival stalks the pages of the book long after his death and presides over the dinner at Hampton Court. In *Fire on the Mountain*, Nanda Kaul has more or less overcome the humiliation of her erstwhile mechanical existence and the sting of remembrance is somewhat softened in the peaceful Kasauli atmosphere. Yet her attitude is the result of that very existence and it is something she cannot escape.

There is a sense of continuity in the passage of time. 'After Monday comes Tuesday, and Wednesday follows.' (*TW*, p. 183) Just as the days follow each other in a cyclic motion, so human life continues. Bernard says in Section 5 of *The Waves* 'My son is born, Percival is dead.' (*TW*, p. 103) Parallel to the cycle of human life is the cycle of days and seasons. In *The Waves*, the cycle of the day is the most obvious but the seasonal cycle is hinted at in the last interlude. 'The tree shook its branches and a scattering of leaves fell to the ground.' (*TW*, p. 159) Here is the typical archetypal situation of death and renewal:

> The trees passively receive the effects of time and flux, they are blown by the wind, but they are also durable, since the seasons make the leaves flourish and then die, only to repeat the cycle again. [12]

In *Fire on the Mountain*, the continuity of life is suggested by Carignano, which brings to mind a lighthouse—solid, stable and lasting, while its different occupants come and go like so many waves in the sea. And like the waves merge into one another, they are absorbed in the long, continuous stream of history. Similarly in *The Waves*, Louis realises that he is part of the historical process. By binding the world in a network of commerce and poetry, he hopes to provide a link of continuity 'to mark this inch in the long, long history that began in Egypt in the time of the Pharaohs, when women carried red pitchers to the Nile.' (*TW*, p. 45)

And now, it would be well to examine how the characters experience time in *The Waves* and *Fire on the Mountain*. In Bernard's summing-up, the note sounded is that of the constant warfare against the enemy, time and here we are reminded of Mrs. Ramsay who in *To the Lighthouse*, also comes up against the same antagonist. Bernard, the representative of the other characters 'becomes the archetype of the race as it struggles with its creative powers against the tyranny of time.'[13] His assertion 'Against you, I will fling myself, unvanquished and unyielding, O Death !' (*TW*, p. 200) strikes a note of affirmation in the novel and reveals the indomitable spirit of man over matter. It is also a triumph of psychological time over clock time. But the novel does not end there. It ends on the note 'The waves broke on the shore.' (*TW*, p. 200) Here the waves represent nature and seem hostile to human aspirations. The final sentence also seems to suggest the triumph of clock time over psychological time and Bernard comes to realise that 'flux is the ultimate reality.' [14]

In *Fire on the Mountain*, Nanda Kaul, like the lotos-eaters wants to drift along the flow of time but fragmented moments of the past impinge upon her consciousness. Ram Lal realises the power of time, ' "She is old, I am old. We are old, old," he muttered, quickly losing hope.' (*FOM*, p. 33) Ila Das struggles against the vagaries of time but submits to its tyranny as it overcomes her in the figure of Preet Singh. At the end of *Fire on the Mountain*, when Nanda Kaul hears of Ila Das's rape and murder, the world of fantasy which she had created for herself falls apart and 'this final confrontation with the truth of her situation, renders her heroic.' [15] But like the final sentence in *The Waves*, here we have the fire on the mountain depicting the triumph of natural over psychological time. It would be significant to note that both *Fire on the Mountain* and *The Waves* end with darkness descending on the scene. *The Waves* ends with the death of Bernard and *Fire on the Mountain* concludes rather violently with the rape and murder of Ila and the death of Nanda Kaul. Hence the setting of the sun signifies the advent of death and dark is the accepted time for sinister happenings.

The Waves and *Fire on the Mountain* leave different effects on the readers because of the difference in technique. Woolf uses recurrent imagery by which she evokes a multiple response in the reader's mind, for example, in the beginning of *The Waves*, we are presented with the image of a ring and a globe. ' "I see a ring" said Bernard.' (*TW*, p. 6) ' "I see a globe," said Neville.' (*TW*, p. 6) This image later finds variations in the images of a knotted handkerchief, a chain, a loop and the purpose of each is to trigger off the reader's response. As Richter says 'the sense of time's passage is evoked through variation of the image by word or meaning,' [16] for example, the ring for Bernard becomes an engagement ring in his youth and in his summing-up it signifies 'The wind, the rush of wheels become the roar of time, and we rushed—where ? And who were we ?" (*TW*, p. 107) It conveys to the reader the futility of human endeavour in the face of eternity. Thus we find the image is repeated, but always with a variation thereby conveying the passage of hours, days and years.

In *Fire on the Mountain*, the image of the plains harks Nanda Kaul back to her distasteful tenure as a wife without identity. Raka like 'a mosquito flown up from the plains,' (*FOM*, p. 40) comes to tantalise her.

Hence, the plains in the distance become for the reader a relic of the past—an image of unrest in contrast to the peace of Kasauli. Desai has created such an indolent atmosphere that the clocks automatically become slower for the reader, as one gets the feeling of being transported to long lazy summer days when no appointments are to be kept or schedules adhered to. While *Fire on the Mountain* is a simple and easily-read book, the complicated set-up of *The Waves* makes it a difficult book by any standards and requires more than one reading to be fully apprehended. Hence, it calls into play the reader's memory so that various sense impressions are related in a composite pattern. Woolf says:

> But memory, after the book is shut, brings out, as sometimes in real life, the details and subtleties which some more salient characteristic has prevented us from noticing at the time.[17]

The technique in *The Waves* is quite different from that of the other novels of Woolf. In the others, we have Woolf's ever-present voice obtruding in the narrative. Here, all we have is a series of quotations introduced by "Bernard said," "said Susan" etc. Commenting on this aspect, Bernard Blackstone says 'In *The Waves* Virginia Woolf carries her mastery, both in thought and technique, to its ultimate point.'[18] The soliloquies are alternated with the lyrical description of nature and this technique is employed to give the sense of the passage of clock time which is sometimes transcended by the characters in moments of vision. Woolf's intention is to present the "moment" whole so that the very texture of life is revealed. Woolf explores the nature of reality:

> Now is life very solid or very shifting ? I am haunted by the two contradictions. This has gone on forever; will last forever; goes down to the bottom of the world—this moment I stand on. Also, it is transitory, flying, diaphanous.[19]

The moment becomes an independent entitv when it combines:

> . . . both physical and mental worlds and engulfing the self in brief ecstatic recognitions before it collapses into its components and burns out like the significant match of Mrs. Woolf's description. Then things become once more external and limiting as the mind

> is wrenched away from objects which it again views as alien and apart from itself.[20]

In *Fire on the Mountain*, the technique is simpler. The chapters in the various sections are scenes and the changes in these scenes constitute the movement in the otherwise static novel. The authorial voice provides all the necessary details. The novelist can be seen passing back and forth between subjective and objective, within the chapter, within the paragraph, within the sentence, for example,

> The postman seemed unable to overtake him hypnotised by the boy's whimsical progress, he stopped and kept behind while Nanda Kaul, slit-eyed burned on the knoll. Hurry man, she mentally snapped—get it over with . . . she could not imagine.
>
> Chapter 2
>
> The postman could imagine nothing but he knew a few things. He had known the house before it was Nanda Kaul's. (*FOM*, p. 5)

Hence we can see the transition from external to internal and then we are taken over smoothly to the next chapter, by the connection formed by the word "imagine." And a bemused authorial voice takes us down the corridors of time to acquaint us with the history of Carignano. Desai makes constant use of the flashback technique so that a multidimensional effect of the passage of time is revealed. It is relevant to stop here and ask why Desai makes use of this technique rather than that of following a chronological sequence. To this the answer would apparently be that she wishes to present the very experience of "life." She does not aim at realism in the sense of clinical adherence to the detail of Zola or the "materialists." It means the presentation of the experience of life and this includes the depiction of human perception of time which is fragmentary, expanding and contracting according to circumstance and having different significance for different people. It is common human experience that the slightest stimulus can cause "involuntary memory" to come into play and we are swamped in a flood of past memories and associations. Hence this frequent recourse to nostalgia gives us a picture of the human mind and its workings. And by her use of memory, Desai has captured the very fluidity of the inner rhythm of life. Desai's technique here is somewhat similar to that used by Woolf in *Mrs. Dalloway*. On the other hand, the technique of *The Waves* strikes one as contrived and artificial and far removed from actual human experience. But it may be argued that the formal style is intended to create an aura of timelessness so that the narrative is removed from the limits of clocks and chronometers.

Woolf's favourite subject is to depict 'the unity and multiplicity, in its relation with the outside world of things and other people,'[21] an idea clearly visible in *Mrs. Dalloway*, *Orlando*, *The Voyage Out* and brought to its utmost refinement in *The Waves*. Like the waves that constantly break from and merge with one another, thus stressing the continuity of the discontinuous, so all human beings are linked together in the chain of time. As Bernard says 'I do not believe in separation. We are not single." (*TW*, p. 46) In the summing-up, he again reiterates 'I am not one person, I am many people, I do not altogether know who I am—Jinny, Susan, Neville, Rhoda or Louis. . . : (*TW*, p. 187) And nowhere is the unity of the personalities more obvious than in the dinner at Hampton Court when all the characters transcend the limits of the ego which are 'extinguished for a moment . . .' (*TW*, p. 187) and become one. As Bernard describes '. . . for one moment out of what measureless abundance of past time and time to come, burnt there triumphant. The moment was all; the moment was enough.' (*TW*, p. 188) But then, the characters draw apart becoming separate entities and hence life once again becomes "transitory, diaphanous" and the sense of eternity is lost. Thus, Woolf's characterisation is much in keeping with her sense of conflict between time and duration, between the transitory and the permanent. She is not trying to depict the character of any one individual as she says vis-a-vis the characterisation of *The Waves* 'But who is she ? I am very anxious that she should have no name. I don't want a Lavinia or a Penelope. I want "she." '[22] So, we can see that her aim is to distil the very essence of human existence.

In *Fire on the Mountain*, the problem is the very opposite. Here the essential loneliness of the individual is stressed. Desai was not interested in "character types" but she depicts individuals as separate entities each with their own special problems. Though Woolf depicts Jinny, Susan, Rhoda, Neville, Louis, Percival and Bernard as each having his or her special hallmark, yet what is stressed is that all these characters are different aspects of the same being. In *Fire on the Mountain*, in spite of the difference in age and situation, all three characters share the same problem of loneliness. Nanda Kaul's problem is that she cannot reconcile illusion and reality and this is beautifully depicted:

> An eagle swept over it, far below her . . . gliding on currents of air without once moving its great muscular wings which remained in repose, in control. She had wished, it occurred to her. to imitate that eagle—gliding, with eyes closed.
>
> Then a cuckoo called, quite close. . . . She recognised its domestic tone. (*FOM*, p. 19)

She wishes to play the majestic role of the eagle, 'to merge with the pine trees and be mistaken for one,' (*FOM*, p. 4) but domestic duties, this time in the shape of Raka jolt her to the reality of being a domestic cuckoo. She is in constant revolt against the role, which she feels has been foisted upon her and like Rhoda in *The Waves*, she is totally immersed in herself and is unable to communicate with the child. She tries to transcend the world of time and space into one of fantasy, but time triumphs in the end and she comes to realise the futility of her self-erected facades. Raka is a highly reticent child but the look in her eyes reveals the turmoil in her soul. Ila Das is a caricature of a genteel woman fallen on bad days but instead of arousing our contempt, she evokes admiration. By taking us to the innermost recesses of her characters' minds, Desai reveals more with fewer words and from the psyche of the three characters, we find, that the past is never far away.

In *The Waves* when one comes to the question of voice, one is led to ask whether it is merely a display of technical skill or if it is in keeping with Woolf's concept of time and space. To which the answer is not so simple for '. . . to define that voice is to solve the whole problem of *The Waves*. . . .'[23] Though Bernard is the "phrase-maker," the other characters also speak in exactly the same language, full of rhythm, alliteration and repetition. It seems as if it is Woolf speaking throughout the book. Hafley calls it the omniscient viewpoint, a view that Naremore does not accept, saying that the consistency in style suggests 'the underlying equivalence of the various characters.'[24] He further explains:

> More often the voices suggest an intimation of immortality, an eternal presence caught for a moment in a temporal, transient world. . . .[25]

And this view is substantiated in what Bernard says :

> I am at liberty now to sink down, deep, into what passes, this omnipresent, general life. . . . The surface of my mind slips along like a pale grey stream reflecting what passes. (*TW*, p. 76)

The characters seem immune to the passage of clock time for the speech is not adapted to their growth—it remains the same throughout—too sophisticated and learned to be that of everyday use. As children, the characters record their sensations in single sentences which expand into paragraphs as they grow older, but there is no change in diction. Louis says:

> It is difficult not to weep as we sing, as we pray that God may keep us safe while we sleep, calling ourselves little children. (*TW*, p. 17)

Jinny, recording her sensations prior to and at the time of kissing Louis, says:

> What moved the leaves ? . . . Is he dead ? I thought, and kissed you, with my heart jumping under my pink frock like the leaves, which go on moving, though there is nothing to move them. (*TW*, p. 9)

A child recording such complex emotion with such alacrity is hardly plausible and gives one the feeling of a Self outside the Self, i.e. an overseeing Self, that observes the sensation of the six characters. This Self cannot be identified with either Jinny or Louis or Neville, but is a compound of all six as in Bernard's words 'The human voice has a disarming quality—(We are not single, we are one).' (*TW*, p. 46) The characters, while not conversing with one another are aware of each other's presence. Susan tells Bernard 'I saw her kiss him.. And I am squat, Bernard, I am short' (*TW*, p. 10) to which Bernard responds 'I saw you go. . . ." (*TW*, p. 10)

In *Fire on the Mountain*, we can hear the omniscient narrator throughout. While silence, rather than speech is the dominant note, we are exposed to snatches of conversation between Nanda Kaul and Raka where the latter responds mostly in gesture rather than speech. Ila Das's strident voice, with its exuberance is italicised when she gushingly stresses particular words 'We haven't met for *ages* dear. . . .' 'It keeps me *sooo* busy.' (*FOM*, p. 21) Through Nanda Kaul's musings, the Vice-Chancellor's house in the dusty Panjab plains is recreated for us and we come to the conclusion that it is through the mind of human beings that the dimensions of time and space are created. When told of Ila's death, Nanda Kaul dropped the telephone:

> With her head still thrown back, far back she gasped: No, no, it is a lie ! No it cannot be. It was a lie—Ila was not raped, not dead. It was all a lie, all. She had lied to Raka, lied about everything. Her father had never been to Tibet. (*FOM*, p. 145)

Time, which had always meandered for Nanda Kaul, here acquired an urgency and speed to match the emergency of the moment like a rapid montage. This serves as an example of the consistency of style and event.

While Woolf's style is studiously literary, much in keeping with her intellectual Bloomsbury background, Desai's style is more casual and consistent with the spirit of modern times. The styles of both authors have been called poetic—and it is easy to see why both make use of suggestion rather than description. While the concept of time of both Woolf and Desai fits in with the definitions of Bergson and Proust, we cannot detect a conscious effort to reconcile time and duration or to project the triumph of one over the other. For, like in life, there are no harsh black and white outlines but intermediate amorphous shades, often merging. Similarly, the concept of time remains an elusive fluid entity, one that is best experienced rather than defined.

NOTES

1. Virginia Woolf, *A Writer's Diary* (London, 1953), p. 105.
2. Ibid., p. 76.
3. J. Guiguet, *Virginia Woolf and Her Works* (London, 1965), p. 281.
4. *A Writer's Diary*, p. 102.
5. R. Freedman, *The Lyrical Novel* (New Jersey, 1966), p. 269.
6. Woolf, quoted in Guiguet, p. 290.
7. Ibid., p. 281.
8. S. Anant, "Anita Desai's *Fire on the Mountain*," *The Journal*

of Indian Writing in English, Vol. 19, No.1, Jan. 1981.

9. J.F. Stewart, "Existence and Symbol in *The Waves," Modern Fiction Studies*, Vol. 18, No. 4, Winter 1972-73, p. 445.

10. R.S. Sharma, *Anita Desai* (New Delhi, 1981), p. 120.

11. R. Rao, *The Novels of Anita Desai* (Ludhiana, 1977).

12. M. Payne, "The Eclipse of Order: The Ironic Structure of *The Waves," Modern Fiction Studies,* Vol. XV, No.2, Summer 1967, p. 211.

13. J. Graham, "Time in the Novels of Virginia Woolf," *Critics on Virginia Woolf*, ed. Latham (Florida, 1970), p. 37.

14. Payne, p. 366.

15. Shanta Acharya, "Problems of the Self in the Novels of Anita Desai," *Language Forum*, Vol. 7, April 1981-March 1982, p. 248.

16. H. Richter, *Virginia Woolf: The Inward Voyage* (New Jersey, 1978), p. 69.

17. Virginia Woolf, *The Common Reader* (London, 1968), p. 212.

18. B. Blackstone, ed., *The Waves* (London, 1977), cover.

19. *A Writer's Diary*, p. 141.

20. Freedman, p. 199.

21. Guiguet, pp. 286-287.

22. Woolf, quoted in Guiguet, p. 285.

23. Guiguet, p. 284.

24. J. Naremore, *The World Without A Self* (New Haven, 1973), p. 160.

25. Ibid., p. 166.

CONCLUSION

Virginia Woolf was often referred to as "highbrow," a term imported from America by H.G. Wells. The appellation is somewhat justified if one considers the fact that the very air Woolf breathed, was steeped in intellectualism. With her Bloomsbury background, she was able to savour the current of the exciting new concepts that were associated with the names of Freud, Bergson, Proust and the Impressionists, to name a few. While not subscribing to any particular ideology, Woolf was directly or indirectly influenced. Rejecting traditional methods of fiction, Woolf's preoccupation was with the depiction of what she terms "life itself,"[1] in other words, ordinary everyday experiences of the individual rather than the sensational or the momentous. Her focus on the workings of the human mind, makes her adopt a technique that takes the reader "under the surface" for a glimpse of the will-o'-the-wisp reality.

Anita Desai, a prominent and up-coming Indian English writer has chosen English, a second language to her, as the medium for the "exploration of sensibility." It is only the use of certain native words like "*Sardar ji*" and "*Sala, suar ka baccha*" that betrays her Indian origin, for her use of the language excels that of some of the British writers themselves. While retaining her originality, Desai is representative of the present trend in Indian English fiction. For purposes of convenience, the trends in this still-burgeoning tradition, may be broadly characterised into three phases. Early Indian English writers concentrated on the theme of the struggle for independence. In the second phase, the focus shifted to the East-West confrontation, with the Western-educated hero facing the problem of accommodation in an Eastern ambience. Recently the trend is to turn more and more inwards and deal with the individual's problems, mostly of an existential nature.[2] Desai's novels fall within this last category though in *Bye, Bye Blackbird*, the Occidental-Oriental encounter is also depicted.

Apart from sharing views on the concept of time, Woolf and Desai have some other similarities that are too strong to be ignored. Both authors give primary importance to the depiction of female characters. Among Woolf's gallery, we have striking portraits of Clarissa Dalloway, Mrs.

Ramsay, Isa Oliver, Katherine Hilbery, to mention a few. The male counterparts Richard Dalloway, Mr. Ramsay and Giles Oliver are at best anaemic and often pompous and priggish without the touch of human warmth, so essential to a vibrant character. I have not included names from *The Waves* for the reason that they are not individual characters but facets of the same personality. In Desai too, the men like Gautama, Bakul, Raman, are no more than counterfoils to offset the female protagonists Maya, Nanda Kaul, Sarah Sen, Sita, Bimla and Tara. In *Fire on the Mountain*, Ram Lal the cook and the postman are the only minor male characters who appear, for the Vice-Chancellor is only sketched from Nanda Kaul's point of view. Their choice of female characters seems to point to the fact that for them the "female of the species" represented the creative principle of life while the male is symbolic of the intellect and dry facts.

Even on the question of marriage, Woolf and Desai appear to hold similar views. In *The Waves*, though both Susan and Bernard are married (to different people), no comment on marriage crystallises. But in *Mrs. Dalloway, To The Lighthouse* and *Between the Acts*, there are three couples, the Dalloways, the Ramsays and the Olivers respectively, who never achieve total union. 'Mismated, solitary, the man and the woman pursue their separate dreams without coming together except "between the acts" and in a kind of confrontation.'[3] Clarissa, for all her love of life, felt, as she mounted to her lonely attic room, that she lacked something.

> It was something central which permeated, something warm which broke up surfaces and rippled the cold contact of man and woman, or of women together. (*MD*, p. 36)

Marriage does not solve the problem of the fundamental solitude of the individual. Maya, who cannot communicate with the cold Gautama, laments 'He was not on my side at all, but across a river, across a mountain, and would always remain so.' (*CTP*, p. 114) Nanda Kaul in *Fire on the Mountain*, is as deeply scarred as the ancient trees that surround her, on account of her loveless marriage. In *Clear Light of Day*, Bakul is insensitive to the finer nuances in Tara's personality while in *Where Shall We Go This Summer ?*, Sita and Raman are hardly compatible in the sense that their mythological namesakes are. In the works of both, the male and the female stand isolated in a typically

Kiplingesque situation where "never the the twain shall meet."

In Woolf's day, female suffrage was still a distant dream and highly opposed by men. Says Richard Dalloway in *The Voyage Out*, ' . . . .Well ! may I be in my grave before a woman has the right to vote in England !' (*TVO*, p. 39) In the face of such chauvinism, Woolf wrote *Three Guineas* and *A Room of One's Own* and was promptly accused of being a militant feminist. But as Ruth Gruber remarked, Woolf cannot forgive women who adopt a "warrior attitude."[4] Her women like Clarissa Dalloway, Mrs. Ramsay, Susan, Jinny and Rhoda are hardly feminists, the only exception being Mary Datchet in *Night and Day*. It is easy to see that Woolf condemns the rigid and fanatical attitude of people like Doris Kilman in *Mrs. Dalloway*. Woolf did not find feminism aesthetically acceptable and her concern is not with any movement but with womanhood as a whole. Similarly, Desai, though not a feminist, is aware of the peculiar plight of Indian women writers:

> . . . they live mostly in such confined spheres and therefore their field of observation is at the same time more restricted and more intense. This leads to their placing their emphasis on a different sense of values. Whereas a man is concerned with action, experience and achievement, a woman writer is more concerned with thought, emotion and sensation.[5]

Desai too is only interested in individuals. Her female characters are sensitive human beings, driven to the limits of despair and living within a confined conventional structure. Her characters do seem to offer an oblique comment on the sad lot of the Indian woman. In *Clear Light of Day*, Mira masi offers an example of child marriage. She is a symbol of the Indian widow, who is discarded by society and held responsible for her very predicament. In *Fire on the Mountain*, Nanda Kaul looks on helplessly as her husband carries on a life-long affair with a Christian woman, whom he cannot marry because of religious taboos. Our authors were/are not living in a vacuum and if they do depict the social condition they do not, *ipso facto*, become slogan-shouting feminists.

Woolf and Desai vividly depict the landscapes of their respective countries. Jacques-Émile Blanche, one of Woolf's perceptive French critics, disregards Proust's influence on her saying that she was far too English to be side-tracked into external lures. He regarded her as having her 'roots deep in the classics of her country.'[6] The British novel cannot be separated from its geographical context. We have 'glittering many pointed and many domed London' and the sound of the sea is never far away—the waves blending one into another in a cosmic continuum. Desai is basically a city novelist, revealing the tensions of surviving in the cosmopolitan jungles—Bombay, Calcutta and Delhi. But she is equally adept in presenting nature like the Kasauli landscape that is the "objective correlative" for Nanda Kaul's mental states and we find the distinction between the nature of man and Nature itself disappearing in a Wordsworthian communion. In *Clear Light of Day*, Old Delhi, steeped as it is in tradition, is symbolic of the presentness of the past while New Delhi stands for the future and the forces of progress. Hence the paradox of Old and New India is presented. Desai's fiction is loaded with typically Indian imagery—the Kathakali dancer, the peacock and above all that inescapable Indian experience—the duststorm, that recurs in most of Desai's works. In *Cry, the Peacock*, the duststorm. in a diabolic gesture, sweeps away Maya's sanity while in *Fire on the Mountain*, it implicitly warns of the final fire. When the duststorm rages over Kasauli:

> 'The hamam will be knocked over !' Ram Lal yelled. . . .
> 'Will it set fire to the garden ?' shouted Raka. . . .
> 'This is how forest fires do start.' (*FOM*, p. 53)

In *Clear Light of Day*, the duststorm blows as long as Bim struggles with her feelings for Raja, and subsides when she is finally able to see as if by 'the clear light of day' that she could feel nothing but love for him and her family for 'No other love had started so far back in time and had had so much time in which to grow and spread.' (*CLD* p. 165) In both the authors, the landscape is not just a setting, it is an environment.

As for religious opinions, Woolf was a professed atheist. In *The Voyage Out*, Rachel Vinrace somewhat echoes Woolf when she tells us that after her visit to church 'She rejected all that she had implicitly believed.' (*TVO*, p. 234) In *The Waves*, conventional religion is ridiculed, and the church service becomes a meaningless ritual "unwarmed by imagination" and when it ends, Bernard thankfully says 'At last . . . the growl ceases.' (*TW*, p. 24) Desai's views on the subject can only be deduced from her works. From *Cry, the Peacock* and her comment on the albino priest, one can detect her disapproval of dogmatic and convention-bound religion. Nowhere in *Fire on the Mountain* and *Clear Light of Day* is either religion or God mentioned and in *Voices in the City*, Kali is not bountiful but a symbol of death and destruction. *Where Shall We Go This Summer ?* also derides the quackery prevalent among the so-called men of God and gives a clue to Desai's views on the subject.

Woolf and Desai have been variously referred to as painters with words and their delight in sensuous imagery brings poetry to the realm of prose. They share the "camera-eye" technique which includes frequent use of flashbacks, cuts, change of focus, the author moving in and the narrative proceeding at different levels of consciousness, for example, the *Boeuf en daube* dinner of Mrs. Ramsay has the author installing herself in one consciousness after the other. In *Clear Light of Day*, though the lives of the Das family are reconstructed through the points of view of Tara and Bim, the author is never far away. In the works of Woolf, there is hardly any logical construction, but a kind of "psychological ragtime" as Max-Pol Fouchet has said.[7] Desai also tries to capture the incoherence that constitutes the fabric of life and this gives her work 'an evanescent quality . . . something like a discreet, whispering overheard note in music.'[8] While there is some similarity, the techniques of both the authors bear their own special hallmark.

From the present study, it is clear that both Woolf and Desai violate chronological sequence in an imitation of life itself. Chronological time cannot imprison the mind which flits back and forth from present to past and back again without any apparent logical sequence. Their technique consists in bringing the reader face to face with what is happening in the present moment. 'In reality, consciousness, is the sum of a momentary present and an endless past.'[9] Woolf and Desai are concerned with qualitative time rather than quantitative time. Both have a shrewd consciousness of time and of man's freedom to move at will in the past, present and future. To this extent they seem to share the concepts of time with Bergson, Proust and his precursor Novalis. Among the twentieth century writers, we have Joyce and Faulkner renouncing the traditional notion of an irreversible time. Just as seventeen hours reconstruct the whole life of Clarissa Dalloway, so the twenty four hours in the life of Leopold Bloom are a comment on the life of humanity. Faulkner's comment 'there is no such thing . . . as was, because the past is,'[10] speaks volumes on the presentness of the past. Faulkner's concept, however, is different from that of Eliot's in "Burnt Norton" where time past and time present are perhaps contained in time future. 'For Faulkner there is only time past which erupts violently into time present and there is no time future.'[11] In Kafka and Camus time is a repetitive, cyclic continuum, 'where struggles and conflicts are transpersonal and primordial, ranging far beyond the life and death of the individual.'[12] In both Woolf and Desai, events take place within space and time. But these events are dependent upon a particular consciousness which establishes its own spatial and temporal dimensions.

In her essay "Poetry, Fiction and the Future," Woolf says:

> That the age of the earth is 3,000,000,000 years, that human life lasts but a second; that the capacity of the human mind is boundless . . . that all bonds of union seem broken, yet some control must exist.[13]

A similar sentiment is expressed by Gautama in *Cry, the Peacock:*

> This life you speak of, this little episode, this brief flash-in-the-pan, how insignificant and trivial it appears compared with this immortal cycle to which all humanity is bound. . . . (*CTP*, p. 122)

Since human life is so insignificant compared with the timelessness of time, the only way to wrest significance out of our existence is that, through the exercise of the mind and imagination, we can recreate time in our own image—and that is the closest that mortals can get to immortality. And this once again brings Proust to mind.

While some similarity exists between the concepts of time of Woolf and Desai with that of Bergson, this connection cannot be exaggerated. In Bergson's view time can be heard as 'the uninterrupted melody of our inner life,'[14] human duration is not a continuity for either of our authors but rather an assembly of isolated moments, called up at random by the imagination. In *Clear Light of Day* Bim says:

> Isn't it strange how life won't flow, like a river, but moves in jumps, as if it were held back by locks that are opened now and then to let it jump, forwards in a kind of flood ? (*CLD*, p. 42)

Memory may salvage the past for us, but all the same something is lost that cannot be retrieved and this something is a feeling of profound loss that we associate with the passage of time. Bim says:

> 'Youth ? . . . I never wish it back. I would never be young again for anything.'
>
> An invisible cricket by her feet at that moment began to weep inconsolably. (*CLD*, p. 43)

The cry of the cricket seems to be a lament for the days gone by and it is reminiscent of Lily Briscoe's cry "Mrs. Ramsay ! Mrs. Ramsay !" Neither of these is a *recherche du temps perdu* but they underscore the fundamental sadness that underlies the human condition. The future soon becomes the past and brings with it a sense of yet more deprivation.

But this does not mean that the novels end on a note of despair. In Woolf's *Mrs. Dalloway* and *To The Lighthouse*, the final vision is that of mind triumphing over matter, while *The Waves* ends on an ambiguous note that the final sentence introduces. In *Cry, the Peacock*, Maya's final leap to death may be viewed as Septimus' opting out of the flow of time. At the close of *Fire on the Mountain*, Nanda Kaul's experience of facing the truth lasts only a moment but this realisation of that moment is eternal. *Clear Light of Day* ends with Bim willing to face the future in an optimistic state of mind.

The significance of the moment is different in *The Waves* from that of *To The Lighthouse* and *Mrs. Dalloway*. While in the latter two novels, the moment is received passively, in *The Waves* we have man as the creator of the moment. Bernard says 'We are creators. We too have made something that will join the innumerable congregations of past time.' (*TW*, p. 104) This sense of the continuity of history is found in Woolf's *Orlando*, *The Years* and *Between the Acts* and also in Desai's *Clear Light of Day*. In *Cry, the Peacock*, it is time chalking out Maya's destiny but in *Clear Light of Day* it is Bim who transcends the bitterness of the past, paradoxically, by delving into the past. In *Fire on the Mountain*, the moment of realisation creates something permanent in the flux of time. In both novelists, the conflict is not between mind time and linear time, nor is there an effort to establish the supremacy of the one over the other. What is stressed is that there is a central relationship between the two worlds that is inseparable from and crucial to human experience.

Hence, life and death are two inseparable facts of human existence. Death, the physical fact is subservient to the time of clocks and chronometers but the question of life and living is entirely a matter of human creativity. Living amidst uncertainty, what becomes important for the individual is his subjectivity—how he is able to apprehend the truth of his existence, and it is this apprehension that enables him to leave "footprints on the sands of time."

Even a passing acquaintance with the works of Woolf reveals her preoccupation with the moment. In the words of Eleanor:

> She felt that she wanted to enclose the present moment; to make it stay; to fill it fuller and fuller, with the past, the present and the future, until it shone, whole, bright deep with understanding. (*The Years*, p. 80)

Ralph Freedman comments 'The moment is the artist's awareness of significant cognitions between his private sensibility and appropriate facts in the outer world.'[15] For though the moment is indeed a subjective experience, it examines the relationship of the mind with external facts. Thus in the works of Woolf, we find a mosaic of moments sewn together by memory the capricious seamstress who

> runs her needle in and out; up and down; hither and thither. We know not what comes next, or what follows after. Thus, the most ordinary movement in the world, such as sitting down at a table and pulling the inkstand towards one, may agitate a thousand odd, disconnected fragments, now bright, now dim, hanging and bobbing and dripping and flaunting like the underlinen of a family on a line in a gale of wind. (*Orlando*, p. 49)

In Desai's works, memory plays the same role. Here the keynote is nostalgia. While the focus is on nostalgia, hope is not obliterated. For both memory of the past and hope for the future are the modes by which we perceive time. Here the author's time sense is that of the reader's. This time balance gives the reader a sense of average reality and suspends the need for chronology or linear plots.

Woolf's innovations came in for a lot of criticism from her contemporaries. But in her experiments she

> never lost sight of her human responsibility as an artist to communicate with her fellow creatures, never allowed herself to stray off arrogantly into a private world, never willingly left her meaning obscure,[16]

and this constitutes her greatness as a committed writer. While some social issues in her novels may appear outdated, her concern with basic human problems lends a quality of timelessness to her fiction. Human experience has remained unchanged through the centuries and life is still a series of ordinary feeling, hopes, despairs and memories that it was years ago. Woolf offers no facile solutions to the question of "What is Life ?" What she offers instead is a glimpse of the moment of vision whereby the reader can share for the moment with the author, a sense of that reality which is too elusive to be trapped n definitions.

This elusive quality is also a hallmark of Desai's fiction, whose focus is on the inner experience of life. But this does not lead her to sacrifice the truth of life in favour of fantasy. She expresses a 'uniquely Indian sensibility that is yet completely at ease in the mind of the West.'[17] Underlying her work, is the feeling of the terrible isolation of the individual and it is this that strikes a sympathetic chord in the sensitive reader. And perhaps it is this quality that will survive the test of time.

NOTES

1. Virginia Woolf, *The Captain's Death Bed and Other Essays* (London, 1950), p. 29.

2. Meenakshi Mukherjee, *The Twice-Born Fiction* (New Delhi, 1974).

3. M. Nathan, *Virginia Woolf* (London, 1961), p. 84.

4. J.B. Batchelor, "Feminism in Virginia Woolf" in *English*, Vol. XVII, No.97, Spring 1968, p. 2.

5. R.S. Sharma, *Anita Desai* (New Delhi, 1981), p. 17.

6. Georges-Paul Collet, "Jacques-Emile Blanche and Virginia Woolf," *Comparative Literature*, Vol.17, 1965, p. 79.

7. Quoted in Nathan, p. 126.

8. M.L. Raina, "An Arid Exercise" in *Indian Book Chronicle*, Vol. VII, No.19, Oct. 1,1982, p. 325.

9. Raj Kumar, *Technique of the Modern Psychological Novelist* (Ludhiana, 1956), p. 28.

10. Lewis P. Simpson, "The Southern Recovery of Memory and History," in *Sewanee Review*, Vol. 82, 1974, p. 2.

11. E.L. Rodrigues, "Time and Technique in *The Sound and The Fury*" in *The Literary Criterion*, Vol. 6, No. 4, Summer 1965, p. 63.

12. M.A. Goldberg, "Chronology, Character and the Human Condition: A Re-appraisal of the Modern Novel" in *Criticism*, Vol. V, No. 1, Winter 1963, p. 11.

13. D.L. Higdon, *Time and English Fiction* (London, 1977) p. 125.

14. Nathan, p. 117.

15. Ralph Freedman, *The Lyrical Novel* (New Jersey, 1966), p. 162.

16. Quoted in Dorothy Brewster, *Virginia Woolf* (London, 1963), p. 171.

17. Peter Alcock, "Rope, Serpent, Fire: Recent Fiction of Anita Desai" in *The Journal of Indian Writing in English*, Vol. 9, No.1, Jan. 1981, p. 33.

ABBREVIATIONS USED

AWD	:	A Writer's Diary
CLD	:	Clear Light of Day
CTP	:	Cry, the Peacock
FOM	:	Fire on the Mountain
JR	:	Jacob's Room
MD	:	Mrs. Dalloway
MFS	:	Modern Fiction Studies
TTL	:	To the Lighthouse
TW	:	The Waves

BIBLIOGRAPHY

A. PRIMARY SOURCES:

Anita Desai. *Bye, Bye Blackbird.* (New Delhi, 1971).
________. *Clear Light of Day* (Harmondsworth, 1981).
________. *Cry, the Peacock* (New Delhi, 1980).
________. *Fire on the Mountain* (New Delhi, 1977).
________. *Voices in the City* (New Delhi, 1982).
________. *Where Shall We Go This Summer ?* (New Delhi, 1982).
Virginia Woolf. *Between the Acts* (London, 1978).
________. *Jacob's Room* (London, 1977).
________. *Mrs. Dalloway* (Harmondsworth, 1976).
________. *Night and Day* (London, 1978).
________. *Orlando* (London, 1979).
________. *The Voyage Out.* (London, 1978).
________. *The Waves* (London, 1979).
________. *The Years* (London, 1979).
________. *To the Lighthouse* (Harmondsworth, 1972).

B. SECONDARY SOURCES:

Béja, M., ed. Virginia Woolf's *To the Lighthouse* (London, 1970).
Bennett, Joan *Virginia Woolf: Her Art as a Novelist* (Cambridge, 1964).
Brewster, D. *Virginia Woolf* (London, 1963).
Edwards, P., ed. *The Encyclopaedia of Philosophy,* Vols. I & VIII (London, 1967).
Freedman, R. *The Lyrical Novel* (New Jersey, 1966).
Frye, N. *Anatomy of Criticism* (New Jersey, 1973).
Golding, *Free Fall* (New York).
Grass, Gunter. *The Tin Drum,* tr. Ralph Manheim (New York, 1961).
Grebstein, S.N. ed. *Perspectives in Contemporary Criticism* (New York, 1965).
Guiguet, J. *Virginia Woolf and Her Works,* tr. Jean Stewart (London, 1965).
Higdon, D.L. *Time and English Fiction* (London, 1977).

Jameson, F. *Marxism and Form* (New Jersey, 1971).
Kannabiran, V. *The Marxist Theory of Fiction* (Unpublished M.Litt. Dissertation, CIEFL, Hyderabad).
Karl, F.R. *A Reader's Guide to the Contemporary English Novel* (London, 1963).
Kettle, A. *An Introduction to the English Novel* (London, 1976).
Kumar, Raj *Technique of the Modern Psychological Novelist* (Ludhiana, 1956).
Latham, J.E.M., ed. *Critics on Virginia Woolf* (Florida, 1970).
Lee, H. *The Novels of Virginia Woolf* (London, 1977).
Lerner, L. *The Uses of Nostalgia* (London, 1972).
Lukacs, G. *The Theory of the Novel* (London, 1978).
McLaurin, A. *Virginia Woolf: The Echoes Enslaved* (Cambridge, 1973).
Majumdar, R. and McLaurin, A., ed. *Virginia Woolf: The Critical Heritage* (London, 1975).
Marder, H. *Feminism in Art: A Study of Virginia Woolf* (Chicago, 1972).
Moody, A.W. *Virginia Woolf* (London, 1963).
Mukherjee, Meenakshi *The Twice-Born Fiction* (New Delhi, 1974).
Nathan, M. *Virginia Woolf*, tr. Herma Briffault (London, 1961).
Naremore, J. *The World Without a Self* (New Haven, 1973).
Prasad, M. *Anita Desai: the Novelist* (Allahabad, 1981).
Rao, B.R. *The Novels of Anita Desai* (Ludhiana, 1977).
Richter, H. *Virginia Woolf: The Inward Voyage* (New Jersey, 1978).
Rosenthal, M. *Virginia Woolf* (London, 1979).
Ruddick, L. *The Seen and the Unseen: Virginia Woolf's To the Lighthouse* (London, 1977).
Sharma, R.S. *Anita Desai* (New Delhi, 1981).
Sprague, C., ed. *Virginia Woolf: A Collection of Critical Essays* (New Jersey, 1971).
Woolf, Virginia *A Writer's Diary* (London, 1953).
________. *The Captain's Death Bed and Other Stories* (London, 1950).
________. *The Common Reader* (London, 1968).